The Narrative Universe

Tabletop Role-Playing Game

Base Edition

Created By: **Written By:**

Joshua Orsak   Daisy Stridinger

Edited by: Ryan Mossbargar
With Artwork from: Anderson Carman

© 2023 Joshua Orsak & Kurt Stridinger
302 S Blackwell St, La Porte, Tx 77571
ISBN: 979-8-88940-173-5

Foreword from the author

Thank you for supporting our *nu* TTRPG project!
(Don't worry, there's plenty more of that throughout the book)

While this book may be new, this system has been played by hundreds of people within the Orsak Narrative Universe for years. Each person who has played has left a lasting impact on the game and helped shape it into what it is today. Now it is our goal to present this system in a comprehensive manual so you can take it and tell stories of your own.

Presented in this PDF is everything you need to begin playing games within the Narrative Universe TTRPG system. Unfortunately, not presented in this PDF is artwork or other trimmings of a professionally published TTRPG manual. Like the ONU community itself, this book has been a labor of love.

The artwork presented in this book has all been professionally commissioned by the ONU community from artist Anderson Carman and is used here with his permission. The portraits are of characters created by players and played in games within the NU system. They represent just the beginning of the possibilities within the NU.

With this initial PDF, we hope to raise the funds to get the NU TTRPG professionally published, not only expanding on the materials found within this book but also hiring artists to bring the Narrative Universe to life. With your support, we hope to have a physical, hardcover book available soon!

If you enjoy the content found in this book, consider visiting the Orsak Narrative Universe on Discord and letting us know! There you can find plenty of other material to use in your games, including extra classes, skills, spells, and entire new power systems created by the players of the community over time.

Again, most sincerely, thank you for supporting this project and helping make this book a reality.

We hope you tell some amazing stories!
-Daisy Stridinger

Join the Orsak Narrative Universe Discord for Bonus Classes, Character Sheets, and a 2 week free trial of the NU system!

Table of Contents:

Mac n Cheese - God of Cosmic Chaos

Chapter 1: Welcome to the Narrative Universe

The Narrative Universe is a game crafted, developed, playtested, and expanded by a community of players over nearly 30 years. The NU was created by a group of friends who sought to take what they loved from their favorite sword and sorcery TTRPGs and use it to create a more story-driven and flexible game that could shine across any number of genres.

The NU was originally brought to life by creator and founder Joshua Orsak through the Orsak Narrative Universe text game community - a massive, interconnected narrative spanning hundreds of games and thousands of players, with each game adding to and changing the course of the story.

Now the Narrative Universe is expanding, and we invite you to create your own worlds, have your own adventures, and most importantly, tell your own stories.

What is the NU?

The NU is a narrative heavy mixed 20-sided, 100-sided tabletop role-playing system, but more than that, it is a *game*. A game designed to be fun for *every* player at the table. A game that rewards creativity without interfering unncessessarily. A game where you can participate in one of the oldest human traditions to ever exist…*telling stories together.*

In the Narrative Universe, players at the table each create a unique character of their own design, ready to set out on their adventure. Throughout your journey, you will use your character's Skills and Spells to try to sway the outcome of Fate Rolls in your favor. One player at the table plays the Narrator. It is their job to facilitate the story and interpret the result of any Fate Rolls the other players make.

Some characters are ferocious combatants, others master spellcasters, others still are skilled orators or even simple farmers, and each has a story to tell within the Narrative Universe…

Rule Zero

"Skills are the narrative, the Narrator is the mechanics." This is rule zero within the Narrative Universe. Your character's abilities should always serve the narrative, and not the other way around. Many Skills and Spells have effects that are not specifically defined, and even those that do may be used in a variety of creative ways.

It is up to the players to come up with creative ways of combining and using their Skills, and up to the Narrator to determine how those Skills impact your game and story. Stories in the NU are always changing with the results of Fate Rolls and rarely go where the Narrator expects them to.

Players are encouraged to use their Skills and Spells in new and unique ways, and Narrators are encouraged to embrace that creativity. If a player wants to use two or three Skills in combination, or do something with a Skill not expressly defined in the Skill's description, the Narrator should work with the player to find a satisfying narrative solution. Any situation that gets too complicated can always be resolved with a Fate Roll.

When a player asks their Narrator if they can use a Skill differently than how it is described, instead of the response being "Let's check the rules," the response in the NU should always be "Let's find out!"

Up to Fate

Fate Rolls are a unique mechanic in the NU that separate the success of a character's actions from the outcome of that action. It is possible for the characters to succeed in every Skill Check, and still face a tragic ending. Similarly, it is possible for your characters to fail so far forward that they actually manage to save the day.

A Fate Roll is always made using a 100-sided die (d100), and the outcomes of a roll can vary greatly. Though typically, the higher the result of the Fate Roll, the better the outcome is in favor of the party. It is up to the Narrator to interpret what the outcome means for the mechanics and narrative. Stories in the NU can change drastically with a single fate roll, so the Narrator is encouraged to tell the story *with* the other players at the table rather than *to* them.

There are numerous ways to gain bonuses to your Fate Roll, tipping the odds in your favor. Through successful Skill Checks, creative solutions, and working together as a party, you can help ensure fate stays on your side.

More information about Fate Rolls can be found in **Chapter 9.**

Narrator's Discretion

The Narrator at your table holds a special position among the players. In addition to being responsible for narrating the action of scenes, they are also the player that determines the outcome of any Fate Rolls.

The NU places a great deal of trust in the Narrator to determine what will work best for their game. Optional rules are presented throughout this manual so you can customize your game to your liking.

Rather than slowing your game down to search for mechanics and rules, the Narrator is trusted to make many of those decisions in the present moment. While the Narrator should always work with the other players at the table to tell the story, at certain points, it will become necessary for the Narrator to make a judgment call in order to keep the story moving forward. Consider the following whenever you have to make one of these decisions as the Narrator:

1. Does the decision make narrative sense? While characters are often capable of incredible and supernatural feats, a good story still needs to have real stakes and obstacles[1] for your players to overcome.
2. Does the decision tell a good story? Oftentimes when we are running games, our imaginations get carried away in what we as the Narrator think will make a good story. Don't get so caught up in your own ideas that you forget to listen to the other

---

[1] Don't worry, we'll get into these more later

players at the table and collaborate with them.

3. Is the decision fun for the players? Consequences are a natural result of player actions but remember, no one enjoys being unduly punished at the table. TTRPGs are *games* and everyone at the table should be enjoying themselves.

Setting Agnostic

The Narrative Universe is a setting agnostic system, meaning the manual here is presented without predetermined lore or peoples. Instead, we provide you with all the tools you'll need to build worlds of your own, along with some writing prompts to help you get started!

This manual is focused on sword and sorcery style, fantasy storytelling, but the system can easily be applied to any other genres or setting suiting your game and play style. For extra classes and skills outside the fantasy genre, visit the ONU Discord community!

A Modular System

A common phrase you will see throughout this book is "...suiting your game and play style." Many mechanics within the NU are meant to be adapted to fit your individual group. This is one of the reasons we highly recommend having a "Session 0" before beginning your game[2].

Either through adding in more complex mechanics or by leaving nearly everything

up to fate, the NU is designed to fit your group, and not the other way around.

If NU Rule Zero is "Skills are the narrative, and the Narrator is the mechanics," then Rule #1 is "There is no wrong way to play the game, so long as everyone at your table is having fun[3]." Mix and match as many systems and optional rules as you like to create a unique experience for your table!

Quick Start Guide

If your group is experienced with TTRPGs and would like to dive into the system first to get a sense of how the rules function, **Appendix A** contains a Quick Start Guide containing everything you need to know to get started playing right away!

Grezula, the Cardboard Fighter

---

[2] Session 0 is covered more in Chapters 2 & 9

[3] That includes you too, Narrators!

Chapter 2: Playing the Game

The Narrative Universe is a long-form, TTRPG system designed to be played over many game sessions (called a "campaign") to encourage character customization and development. Though a story can be told in a single session of the game (often called a "one-shot"), campaigns allow players to follow a single character's journey from their humble beginnings to their heroic finale.

One player at the table assumes the role of the **Narrator**. The Narrator describes the action of the scene, controls any non-player characters the party encounters on their journeys, and interprets the result of any **Fate Rolls** made. The other players at the table each control a **Character**, making up the party[4]. Characters utilize their **Skills** and **Spells** to overcome any challenges and obstacles the Narrator may throw their way.

Each session is played over several **Rounds**. Rounds typically begin with the Narrator setting the scene and describing the situation the party finds itself in. Each player is given a chance to take an **Action** or respond to the situation, interacting with and changing the direction of the story. Characters will make any appropriate Skill Checks and Fate Rolls from their actions, and the Narrator responds to each roll made. Depending on the outcome, Fate Rolls may change the scene drastically either in the party's favor or against it.

---

[4] Character creation is convered in detail in the next chapter

Session 0

A "Session 0" is a meeting of the players before the first game where they can discuss tone, setting, safety tools, characters, and more!

It is vitally important all players agree upon the style and tone of the story you would like to tell as a group before you begin telling it. It is highly recommended that you hold a Session 0 with your group before you begin your game.

Our full recommendations for what to include in your Session 0 can be found in **Chapter 9.** These include:
- Tone and genre of your game
- The world of your game
- Characters and backstories
- The amount of Combat vs Role-Play
- Safety tools and issues you do not wish to be a part of your game

Types of Rounds

Broadly speaking, rounds in the NU can be broken down into three categories: Preparation, Exploration, and Combat.

Preparation rounds represent in game downtime while the characters are not under direct threat. During this time, every character gets an opportunity to train a Skill, purchase items using **Money Points** they've earned, or **Craft** new pieces of equipment using **Gathering Points**. Additionally, this is a good opportunity for characters to interact with any NPCs in the area to learn new information.

Preparation rounds also offer opportunities for characters to interact with each other outside the stress of combat and exploration, deepening the interpersonal bonds between your characters.

The Narrator may call for a preparation round whenever your party is setting out for a new day of adventuring, has some downtime in a city or settlement, or is traveling from one location to another.

Exploration rounds represent your party exploring new areas or dungeons, and dealing with the dangers of their environment. While there is not enough time to train Skills or craft items, characters may still attempt to learn about their environment or ready themselves for the dangers ahead.

Characters may encounter environmental dangers during exploration rounds, requiring the use of Skills to progress safely. **Exploration encounters** may range from traversing unsafe terrain, such as a rocky cliffside, to run-ins with the local creatures nearby. More information on these types of encounters can be found in **Chapter 7.**

Combat rounds represent a few moments of the conflict, during which each combatant gets an opportunity to take an **Offensive** or **Defensive** action. For some groups combat rounds may be rare, but even the most cautious of parties may find themselves in a situation where they are forced to fight. Combat rounds are described in further detail in **Chapter 8**.

Taking Actions

During each round, characters can take actions to interact with the story. The two primary types of actions are Skills and Spells.

Skills represent the talents and training your characters have at their disposal to help them overcome obstacles. Each character has a list of Skills chosen from their Class's Skill list[5]. During preparation rounds, as well as whenever you gain a level, you can gain new Skills or improve the Skills you already have.

Whenever you use a Skill, you'll roll a Skill Check using a 20-sided die (d20) to determine the outcome. More information about Skills can be found in **Chapter 10.**

Certain classes, like the Mage and Priest, also gain access to powerful magic spells to enhance their abilities. Spells are gained similarly to Skills, but chosen off a separate class list. Spells don't require you to roll a Skill Check but are limited in other ways. Some spellcasters must expend mana to cast their spells, while others are limited by the frequency they may cast each individual spell. Spellcasting is covered in detail in **Chapter 12.**

Skill Checks

Whenever the Narrator presents a situation or encounter to the characters, the characters may respond by stating which Skills they would like to attempt to use to overcome the situation. Skills in the NU are often open-ended and can be creatively applied to any number of situations.

Characters in the NU have 7 unique **Ability Scores** used to determine the outcome of Skill Checks. These Ability Scores are:

---

[5] See Appendix E

- Strength
- Dexterity
- Constitution
- Intelligence
- Wisdom
- Charisma
- Offense Rating

Each Skill has 1 or more **Reliant Abilities** that tell you which ability scores will be used when attempting to use that Skill.

Whenever a character attempts a Skill Check, they roll a d20 for each of the Skills Reliant Abilities The outcome is compared to that character's corresponding ability score using a roll under system.

If the roll is **less** than the character's ability score, the Skill Check is a success. If the roll is **equal** to the ability score, it is considered a critical success. If the roll is **higher** than the ability score, the Skill Check fails.

Many Skills utilize 2 reliant abilities, meaning to use them to their full effectiveness you must succeed a Skill Check for each. If you fail 1 or both of these rolls, that counts as a failure for the Skill Check.

Your character's Skills do not represent the limit of their abilities. If you would like to do something as your character that doesn't correspond to one of your Skills, you may simply tell your Narrator the actions you would like to attempt instead. The Narrator may then ask you to make a Skill Check using any ability they feel suits the action you are attempting. Likewise, for very simple actions - such as opening a stiff door or looking around a crowded tavern for someone - the Narrator may choose which Abilities to roll a Skill Check for.

Fate Rolls

Successfully completing a Skill Check doesn't always guarantee things go well for the characters. Great successes can lead to grave consequences, just as failure can lead to a serendipitous result. Sometimes the outcome of your actions is left up to fate…

Fate Rolls are a unique mechanic in the NU that help the Narrator determine how the actions of the party affect the story. Fate Rolls are made after any Skill Checks have been resolved, and most often occur when a character's actions change the narrative in some way. If Skill Checks determine whether or not the characters are successful, a Fate Roll determines the degree of that success.

Fate Rolls are always made using a d100 (or two 10-sided dice). A high roll means something good happens in the party's favor, while a low roll means further complications towards the party reaching their ultimate goal.

Example: Let's say the party discovers an injured traveler on the side of the road. They decide to stop and attempt to help the traveler. If the party successfully completes any Skill Checks to heal the traveler, but makes a low Fate Roll, the traveler might turn out to be a bandit setting up a trap to lure them closer.

Now let's look at the opposite situation: The party has failed their Skill Checks to heal the traveler, but has made a high Fate Roll. In this scenario, perhaps the traveler's wounds were too serious for the party to heal, and in their last breath the traveler bestows a quest upon the party to return the lockbox they were carrying back to the queen.

Bonuses and Penalties

Occasionally, through smart choices or successful Skill Checks, fate can be swayed one way or another. At the Narrator's discretion, they may reward a **Bonus** or impose a **Penalty** on a Fate Roll depending on the circumstances and the choices of the party. Many Skills also grant you a Bonus towards a Fate Roll on a successful Skill Check, but be careful. Failing the Skill Check means you will take a Penalty to the Fate Roll instead.

There are many options for modifying Fate Rolls with Bonuses and Penalties. These are covered further in **Chapter 9,** and you should discuss which option works best for your game during Session 0. We recommend beginning with each Bonus adding 5 to the outcome of a Fate Roll, and each Penalty subtracting 5 instead.

It is also possible to gain a Bonus to a Skill Check, however these function differently than Bonuses to Fate Rolls. Rather than add a number to the outcome of the roll, you increase the Skill Check's Reliant Ability by 2 to determine a successful outcome.

Example: During an exploration round, our party is attempting to climb a steep mountain. One of the party members purchased a Climbing Toolkit, which grants them a Bonus to any Climbing Skill Checks. Using their Toolkit while attempting to scale this mountain would increase their effective Strength score by 2 points, making it easier for them to succeed in any Skill Checks.

Certain Bonuses granted by Skills may be more esoteric and enhance the character's abilities in other ways. In these situations, it is up to the Narrator to determine any specific bonuses granted to either Skill Checks or Fate Rolls.

Vic, the Worm-man
(or at least 1 of them)

Chapter 3: Character Creation

The character you play represents your personal window into the Narrative Universe, the figure within the game you will take control over and make decisions for.

The NU is a system designed to adapt and fit whatever story your group would like to tell. This includes any type of character you want to create, from traditional fantasy archetypes like the elven mage to giant, sentient dung beetles and tugboats with legs. The characters you can create are only limited by your imagination.

The people your party plays and interact with in the world will change drastically depending on the setting and type of game your group is playing. You should discuss the types of characters you would all like to play during session 0.

Detailed here are the general guidelines for creating characters within the Narrative Universe.

Character Description

Before building your character mechanically in the system, first it is important to get an idea of who they are. Begin by describing your character's physical appearance and background.

Worlds within the NU are filled with a rich and diverse variety of people. Unlike other TTRPG systems, there is no predefined list of available races or species you can play, and the physical aspects of your character typically do not mechanically impact the game.

Feel free to choose any of your favorite fantasy staples, such as elves, dwarves, orcs, or create your own. Each of the character portraits contained within this book is a unique character that has been created and played within the Narrative Universe!

The physical aspects of your character are completely up to your interpretation, although all players are encouraged to build characters that will fit within the story and alongside the other party members.

Alternative: At the Narrator's discretion, you may switch one of your 3 starting Skills for a Skill that suits the physical aspects of your character. For instance, if your character has wings, your Narrator might allow you to gain the ability to fly in exchange for a starting Skill.

Creating your Backstory

Your character's backstory can play an even larger role in getting to know who they are. Your backstory should explain how your character began adventuring, as well as what brings them to the place where the story will begin. Make your background as long or as short as you feel is appropriate for your game.

While there is no wrong way to create your character, your stories will be much richer and full of detail if you create strong, compelling characters with rich backstories. A strong character here does not refer to a character who is powerful within the world. Rather, it refers to characters with clear motives, strengths, and weaknesses you can use to help portray them throughout your game. This helps you make difficult choices as your character to advance the narrative forward.

While strong characters have strengths they excel at, they also have weaknesses and flaws they must rely on the rest of the party to help with.

Aspects of your character you may want to consider are:
- What beliefs are core to their person?
- What virtues do they hold dear?
- What flaws or shortcomings do they have?
- Where did they grow up?
- Who are the people closest to them?
- Do they worship any of the deities of this world?
- Do they consider themselves a good or a bad person?
- Do others consider them a good or a bad person?
- Do they have any enemies?
- Why is your character adventuring?
- What would make your character *stop* adventuring?

The Narrator should take notes of the character's backgrounds and utilize them in building the story. Tying your story into the characters themselves can be a powerful tool to engage players and tell a compelling story.

Finally, be sure to give your character a fitting name! Now that you know a little about who your character is, we'll begin building them mechanically!

Ability Scores

Your ability scores represent different aspects of your character's physical and mental attributes. There are 6 main abilities in the NU:

- Strength: The measure of your character's physical might.
- Dexterity: Your character's agility and deftness.
- Constitution: How tough your character is.
- Intelligence: Your character's "book-smarts."
- Wisdom: The combined measure of your character's experience, judgment, and intuition.
- Charisma: How eloquent your character is and their force of personality.

Your ability scores are used to determine the outcome of any Skill Check you make. Whenever you make a Skill Check, you will consult that Skill's Reliant Ability, which tells you what Ability scores will be used to determine the outcome of the roll. Some complex Skills utilize a combination of 2 or 3 Reliant Abilities. If a Skill has multiple reliant abilities, roll a different Skill Check for each one.

To determine your starting ability scores roll 8d20. Ignore the lowest two results and record the rest on your character sheet in any order you wish.

Alternative: Your Narrator may allow you to lower your ability scores to gain extra starting Skills. If you wish to use this optional rule, you may gain 1 extra starting Skill for each point you lower any of your ability scores. The Narrator may determine a limit for the total number of times this may be done for each character.

Offense Rating

Every character has an additional ability score called their Offense Rating. This is a combined measure of their training and skills in armed combat. Your character's Offense Rating is determined by their class and increases over time.

Offense Rating works similarly to other ability scores but is primarily used in attacks and Offensive Skills. Whenever you are required to make a Skill Check using your Offense Rating (OR), you must still roll equal to or lower than your score for a success.

To make an attack, you must make a Skill Check using your OR. On a success, you make a Fate Roll and deal damage equal to that percentage of the target's total Health Points. There are many alternative options for determining the damage dealt by atacks found in **Chapter 8.** Choose the one that best suits your game and play style.

Choosing Your Class

Your character's class defines their primary archetype and how they operate within the confines of the game. Each class grants your character access to a list of Skills available for training. Your class also determines your starting Health Points and Offense Rating. Classes are covered in full detail in the following chapter.

After you select your class, write it down on your character sheet. Roll the die found under the Class Stats to determine your starting Health Points. You should note your class's starting OR, as well as your available Mana if you receive any.

Most classes begin with 3 starting Skills or Spells[6]. Select a total of 3 Skills or Spells from your Class's lists and note them on your character sheet. It's helpful to list any Reliant Abilities of a Skill here, as well any notes you may need to quickly reference, such as page number.

Starting Equipment:

Throughout the game, your characters will obtain powerful items and create new ones of their own invention, but everyone has to start somewhere. The equipment your character begins the game with is determined by what class you choose at level 1. List your starting equipment on your character sheet, as well as any other items your Narrator may give you to begin the game.

Your character also begins the game with a small amount of Money Points (MP). "Money Points" is a generic term for the total value of any currency or valuable items your characters can sell and trade.

Gathering Points (GP) are used in the crafting of new items, and represent the raw materials you will use to produce a new piece of equipment. You do not begin the game with any Gathering Points, but may spend a preparation round searching for them.

---

[6] Rogues begin with 4 because they're better than you

Advancing your Character

As your story continues, your characters will grow in power and gain access to new Skills and Spells. Rather than use an experience point system, Levels in the NU are granted by the Narrator after significant points in the story.

Whenever you gain a level, roll the die listed for your class's Health Points and permanently increase your total by that amount. You also select 3 Skills or Spells to train. These may be new Skills or Spells chosen from your class lists, or ones you already have but would like to improve. You do not need to roll any Skill Checks to train Skills when you level up as you would during a preparation round.

As long as you have access to spellcasting, you may choose any combination of Skills and Spells while leveling up. Even though Bards have access to spellcasting, because they do not have a spell list they may only choose new Skills while leveling up.
(Note: Rogues gain an additional Skill every time they level up)

At level 10, all characters gain an extra action they may use during each round of an encounter.

Multiclassing

You may choose to multiclass when you level up to gain the benefits from another class for your character. Keep track of any levels you have from classes separately.

When you gain a level in a new class, you gain access to that class's unique Core Ability. You also gain additional Health Points depending on your new class's level.

You gain access to any Skills or Spells on your new class's lists for training. However, you may only take Skills and Spells from a class's list depending on your level in *that* class, not your total level overall.

For example: If you have 3 levels in Fighter and 3 levels in Rogue, you may take Skills as if you were level 3 in both classes, but may not train any Skills requiring you to be level 6 in either.

Grunkle, the Goblownie

Chapter 4: Classes

Are you a brave warrior, wading into the frontlines to protect your allies? Or are you a cunning scoundrel who talks their way through even the most dangerous encounters? Are you a prophet? An artist? A scholar searching for new ways to utilize the flow of magic within this world?

Each class has its own unique Skill list which you may choose freely from, allowing you to build and customize your character in any way you want.

Your class will determine your character's Health Points, Offense Rating, and equipment, and give you access to that class's core ability. A full list of Skills on each class's Skill list is located in **Appendix E**.

Here we present a core group of fantasy themed classes that should hopefully be familiar to those who have played that style of TTRPG before! For additional classes, including those outside of the fantasy genre, visit our Discord!

The classes presented in this chapter are:
- Bard
- Charlatan
- Druid
- Fighter
- Mage
- Priest
- Rogue

Bard

"They're armed with nothing but a lute! Come on, lads, how dangerous could they be?" - Famous last words of Khibel the Bandit King.

Weaving together art and magic, the Bard is an incredibly flexible class with a wide variety of Skills available for them to learn.

While Bards can make use of any ability, they most commonly utilize Charisma in their magical performances.

Class Stats:
Health Points / level: 1d4
Mana / level: 9
Offense Rating: 5, +1 every 3rd level
Skills per level: 3
Starting Equipment:
- 1 musical instrument of your choice
- 1 tool kit of your choice
- 2000 mp

Core Ability: Musical Spellcasting
Unlike other spellcasting classes, Bards do not cast their spells off of a spell list. Instead, when a Bard character casts a spell, the player finds a song they feel matches the effect they want to create with the spell. This can be a song that exists in the real world or one the character makes up on the spot. The effects of a Bard's spellcasting do not have to match the effects of spells listed in **Chapter 13**.

The mana cost of all musical spells is variable. For more information about variable cost spells, see **Chapter 12: Spellcasting.** Generally though, the more mana a Bard puts into their spell, the more powerful its effects. The Narrator may limit the total influence a Bard has over their spells depending on their level.

To determine the effects of a Bard's musical spellcasting, make a Fate Roll and add a bonus equal to the amount of mana spent in the spell's casting. The Narrator may award a Bonus to song choices they feel are a particularly good fit for the situation or effect.

In addition, Bards automatically start with the *Musical Talent* Skill in addition to their other start Skills, listed below.

Musical Talent
Classes: Bard
Action: Special
Reliant Abilities: Wisdom

Bards are such masters of the musical arts that their talents transcend the mortal realm, weaving magic into their songs and stories. Some dedicate their lives to the mastery of a musical instrument, others sing with a voice capable of enchanting the gods. Bards' musical talents are as varied and unique as the bard themself! At level 1, you may pick a particular specialization your bard uses to channel your magic through.

Charlatan
"If ALL of the gods are real, why waste your time praying to just one?"

Shunned from most organized religions, Charlatans levy the assistance of multiple deities of the pantheon, refusing to dedicate themselves to just one. While this grants them a certain degree of flexibility as opposed to other divine spellcasters, Charlatans must accept the risk that their prayers may go unanswered.

While high Wisdom and Intelligence scores will help a Charlatan blend in better with religious organizations, the primary ability they use to appeal for a deity's favor is Charisma.

Class Stats:
Health Points / level: 1d4
Offense Rating: 5, +1 every 4th level
Skills or Spells / level: 3
Starting Equipment:
- A set of robes
- 3 holy symbols of their choice
- 250 mp

Core Ability: Fallible Prayers
Charlatans' spellcasting ability functions like the Priest class's Prayers, although with an added risk of failure. In exchange, Charlatans are not bound by one particular deity's tenants, and do not have to follow a holy writ. Charlatans gain a number of Skills allowing them to seek aid from multiple celestial beings.

Whenever you cast a spell as a Charlatan, roll a d100 and consult the table below to determine if you succeed in casting your spell.

Charlatan Level	Spell Failure Range
1-3	40 and below
4-7	33 and below
8-10	25 and below
11-14	15 and below
15-19	10 and below
20+	5 and below

If you roll below your Spell Failure Range, you expend the use of your Prayer but it has no effect.

Charlatans select their Spells off the Prayer list located in **Chapter 13.**

Druid

Stewards and defenders of the natural world, Druids can often be found on the outskirts of society, playing an important role in maintaining the natural balance of the world.

Druids guide their allies through the wilderness with ease, using their Wisdom and Intelligence to read local wildlife and concoct herbal remedies.

Class Stats:
Health Points / level: 1d6
Offense Rating: 5, +1 every 3rd level
Skills or Spells / level: 3

Starting Equipment:
- A staff
- An herbalism tool kit
- 1000 mp

Core Ability: Natural Spellcasting
Druids draw their magical abilities from their connection with the natural world. Because of this, many Druid circles seek out simple lives away from larger cities.

Druids can cast Spells like Priests and select their available Spells from the Prayer list. Druids may also expend the use of one of their Prayers to take on the form of an animal, gaining any natural abilities of their new shape while maintaining their intelligence and personality. You may choose to end the transformation as a free action. Consult the table below to determine what level Prayer you must expend to transform.

Animal form	Spell Level
Small creature	1
Medium creature	3
Large creature	5
Creature with special movement (flying, swimming, burrowing)	4
Magical creatures	*Narrator's discretion

Fighter

Whether they are taking to the front lines to defend their allies, acting as battlefield leaders, or supporting their allies from a distance, Fighters excel in all things combat.

Physical attributes: Strength, Dexterity, and Constitution, are often the most important to a Fighter, though Wisdom and Intelligence can help you survey the battlefield and locate your opponent's weaknesses.

Class Stats:
Health Points / level: 1d10
Offense Rating: 10, +1 every other level
Skills / level: 3
Starting Equipment:
- 1 weapon of your choice

- Light armor and a shield
- Basic traveling tool kit
- 1000 mp

Core Ability: Combat Expertise
Years of training have honed your instincts on the battlefield. During combat encounters, you may take 1 defensive action per round without using your next turn's action.

Mage

Opening themselves up to energies from multiple dimensions of existence, Mages spend their lives in the pursuit of understanding magic. Developing a potent source of energy within themselves, called Mana, Mages are capable of truly wondrous feats.

Intelligence serves well in a Mage's academic studies, while Wisdom is necessary for the careful practice of new spells.

Class Stats:
Health Points / level: 1d4
Mana / level: 9
Offense Rating: 5, +1 every 3rd level
Skills and Spells / level: 3
Starting Equipment:
- A Mage's staff, wand, or amulet
- A small library of spell books in their home location
- 1000 mp

Core Ability: Arcane Spellcasting
Whenever a Mage casts a Spell, they transfer a small portion of their soul to another realm of existence, opening themselves up to the energies there and acting as a conduit to release those energies into the mortal realm. It often takes Mages years to study the proper control of their spells and develop the internal energy source, called Mana, which allows them to do so.

Mages may learn Spells from the Mage Spell list located in **Chapter 13.** Mages must spend Mana to cast their Spells, which is fully restored after a good night's rest[7].

Mages additionally automatically start with the *Research* Skill in addition to their other starting Skills and Spells, listed below.

Research
Classes: Mage
Action: Preparation
Reliant Abilities: Intelligence

Many mages spend years in academia honing their craft, creating new spells, and looking through countless tomes of knowledge while they do so.

During a preparation round, you may attempt a Skill Check to use whatever resources you have to learn more about a particular subject, or craft new spells. On a success, make a Fate Roll to determine the progress you make in your research. If you are in a location where you have access to stores of knowledge, you gain a Bonus on this Fate Roll.

Priest

Often found leading the world's religious organizations, Priests act as agents of the divine pantheon here in the mortal realm. Channeling powerful divine magics through

---

[7] Or whatever your Robot Mage's equivalent is

their Prayers, a Priest can be a beacon of light or a torrent of darkness depending on the deity they serve.

Wisdom is the primary ability Priests use in deciphering the messages their god sends them, along with Intelligence to learn and cast new spells. Charisma also helps a Priest connect with their congregation and spread the message of their deity.

Class Stats:
Health Points / level: 1d4
Offense Rating: 5, +1 every 4th level
Skills and Spells / level: 3
Starting Equipment:
- 1 set of robes
- 1 holy symbol of their deity
- A holy writ from their order
- Healer's tool kit

Core Ability: Divine Prayer
A Priest channels their spellcasting ability through prayers to their deity, creating a direct line to the divine realm and its powers. Their Spells, called Prayers, do not require Mana to cast and instead may be used as frequently as allowed in the Prayer's description. Priests may choose their Prayers off the Priest Spell list located in **Chapter 13.**

These powers, however, come at a cost. Priests automatically start with the *Holy Writ* Skill in addition to their other starting Skills and Spells, listed below.

Holy Writ
Classes: Priest
Action: Enduring Feature
Reliant Abilities: Wisdom, Charisma

You have taken up the tenants of your deity, and in exchange for following them faithfully have been granted extraordinary powers.

When you gain Holy Writ, talk with your Narrator to determine a list of tenants your character must follow that uphold the values of their deity. If you stray too far from your Holy Writ, you may lose access to your Divine Prayers core ability until you reconcile with your deity.

Rogue
Skilled technicians both on and off the battlefield, Rogues excel at using superior tactics to gain the advantage. With a unique toolkit of Skills available only to them, Rogues can often complete jobs with ease that other classes may struggle with.

Dexterity is key to a Rogue's survival on the battlefield and is also used in a number of their Skills. Intelligence and Wisdom can help a Rogue pull off a number of jobs, while Charisma can get them out of a tight spot.

Class Stats:
Health Points / Level: 1d6
Offense Rating: 8 +1 every other level
Skills / level: 4
Starting Equipment:
- 1 weapon of their choice
- Rogue's kit
  - Lockpicking kit
  - Pickpocketing kit
  - Burglary kit
- 2000 mp

Core Ability: Percentage Skills
Rogues gain access to a unique set of Skills that function differently than others. Rather

than relying on their ability scores, these Skills rely on your experience and expertise. Percentage Skills are noted by a numbered percentage in parentheses next to the Skill, which is the Skills starting current percentage.

The Skill's current percentage represents its success rate. When performing a Skill Check with a Percentage Skill, you will roll a d100 instead of a d20. A success is any number equal to or lower than your current percentage on the d100. You can score a critical success on a Percentage Skill by rolling a number directly equal to your current percentage.

Percentage Skills do not have improved levels like other Skills[8]. Instead, you improve them by increasing their current percentage, making it easier to score successes on Skill Checks. To improve your current percentage you may choose to train a Percentage Skill that you already have during a preparation round, or whenever your character levels up.

During a preparation round, you may attempt 5 Skill Checks for your chosen Percentage Skill as usual. Every success increases your current percentage by 1%, and any critical success increases it by 3%.

When leveling up, you may exchange one or more of the 4 Skills you would normally gain to raise the current percentage of any of your Percentage Skills by 1%.

The maximum current percentage for each Skill is listed in the Skills description in **Chapter 10.**

Wangelay -
Technomancer Supreme, box fanatic

---

[8] Improved Skill Levels are detailed in Chaper 10

Chapter 5: Equipment

The tools and equipment your characters carry with them play an important role in both exploration and combat. From weapons and armor to magic potions and scrolls, there are plenty of options for your characters to carry with them on their journeys.

Money Points

The NU uses a system called Money Points to keep track of any gold, jewels, or valuable items the party collects during their adventures. Money Points (mp) represent the total worth of all valuables your character has obtained but is not currently using, and are generally given as a reward for completing jobs or adventures.

Rather than having to sell any valuable items when the party reaches the next town or city, it is assumed they will do so in advance and the party is awarded a flat mp value instead of any miscellaneous items.

MP may be exchanged for goods and services just like other currencies and is often a stand-in for whatever currency your world uses. Depending on your setting, you can easily convert mp to other currencies, such as gold for a fantasy setting or credits for a more science fiction adventure.

Alternative: If your group prefers to play through these sales interactions and keep track of individual items, you are more than welcome to do so! In many cases, the NU presents a more streamlined ruling, but you are always welcome to add however much complexity your group likes.

Economy

While a few items are presented with costs further in this chapter, most items and equipment you will come across are created by the players at your table or the Narrator. Rather than limit players to a select few tables of items and equipment, instead we present a few guidelines for creating items and equipment with your group and setting costs for those items.

The table below is a base recommendation for setting the costs of equipment and items found in your game.

Equipment Level:	Recommended Cost:
Basic	0-1,000 mp
Specialized	1,000-5,000 mp
Artisan	5,000 - 25,000 mp
Wondrous	25,000 - 100,000 mp
Unique	100,000+ mp

Basic: Starting equipment and easily obtainable, everyday items such as rope and camping supplies.
Examples: Chalk - 1 MP, 1 week's worth of rations - 5MP, 100 ft of climbing rope - 250 MP, Winterized tent - 1000 MP

Specialized: Items and equipment that serve a specific purpose, such as thieves' tools or crafting equipment.
Examples: Toolkits - 2500 MP, Alchemy supplies - 3000 MP, Spyglass - 4000 MP

Artisan: Finely crafted ordinary items, often made with specialized materials. These typically grant some kind of bonus compared to non-artisan versions. Examples: Fine jewerly tools - 10,000 MP, 3rd level Spell Scroll - 20,000 MP

Wondrous: Often magical items with extraordinary effects. Examples: Enchanted armor - 75,000 MP, Portable Cottage - 100,000 MP

Unique: One-of-a-kind items, relics, the stuff of legends.

Weapons

Many classes begin with a weapon to use in combat. A "weapon" is broadly defined as any item the character is trained with in combat. This can be anything from your traditional swords and axes to martial arts and frying pans. Rather than individual weapons possessing different properties and dealing differing levels of damage, the damage and effects of your attacks are dependent on the Skills used for the attack.

Most weapons play only an aesthetic role in defining your character and have no direct impact on the mechanics of the game other than if your weapon is ranged or melee.

Alternative: If you and your Narrator like, you may develop unique properties or Skills for your weapons as you see fit. For example, a polearm weapon may be able to strike enemies further away but suffer a Penalty to attack enemies directly next to you.

Weapons of higher quality may grant Bonuses to attacks or damage at the Narrator's discretion.

Armor & Shields

Armor:
Armor in the NU falls into three weight categories: Light, Medium, and Heavy. Each weight category has different benefits and drawbacks described below.

Light Armor (Basic): Simple, lightweight pieces of armor that don't impact your ability to move around.
- Once per encounter, you may roll a d100 and reduce the amount of damage you take by a percentage equal to the result.
- You may use this ability a second time during the same encounter. However, if you do so the armor breaks and must be repaired.
- You may not cast spells or prayers while wearing light armor without the Battle Caster Skill.

Medium Armor (Specialized): Standard equipment for most militaries and town guards, medium armor offers more protection but is more difficult to move around in.
- Once per encounter, you may reduce the damage taken from an attack to 0.
- You may use this ability a second time during the same encounter. However, if you do so the armor breaks and must be repaired.
- You may not cast spells or prayers while wearing medium armor without the Improved Battle Caster Skill.
- You suffer a Penalty to any Fate Roll made while trying to hide your presence while moving.

Heavy Armor (Artisan): Often worn by knights and other paragons on the battlefield, heavy armor offers the most protection at the cost of your mobility.

- Whenever you are hit by an attack, you may roll a d100 and reduce the amount of damage you take by a percentage equal to the result.
- Once per encounter, you may reduce the damage taken from an attack to 0.
- You may use this ability a second time during the same encounter. However, if you do so the armor breaks and must be repaired.
- You may not cast spells or prayers while wearing heavy armor without the Superior Battle Caster Skill.
- Any Dexterity Skill Checks you make while wearing heavy armor are made at half your total Dexterity score.

Shields:

Shields are divided into two categories: Light and Heavy. Each is described below:

Light Shields (Basic/Specialized): Made from wood or other, lighter materials, Light Shields offer their wielder increased protection at the cost of their second hand.

- Once per encounter whenever you would be hit by an attack, you may use a Defensive action to use the Parry Skill. You do not suffer any penalties for being untrained in the Skill while using your shield.
- You may use this ability a second time during the same encounter. However, if you do so the shield breaks and must be repaired.
- Light Shields are light enough to be used as a thrown or melee weapon.

- You may not cast spells or prayers while wearing a shield without the Battle Caster Skill.

Heavy Shields (Specialized/Artisan): Often called kite or tower shields, these heavier shields are often employed by larger militaries and provide enough cover to hide behind.

- Whenever you are hit by an attack, you may use a Defensive action to use the Parry Skill. You do not suffer any penalties for being untrained in the Skill while using your shield. A defensive action used this way always takes your next turn's action, even if you are a Fighter.
- On your turn you may choose to take cover behind your shield. This functions the same as the basic combat action described in **Chapter 8.**

Toolkits

Some classes, such as the Rogue and Bard, and any character who wishes to craft new equipment, will need some trade tools to get the job done.

Tool kits are generally available at the specialized or artisan levels. Whenever a player buys a tool kit, they select one Skill or Craft the kit is designed for.

Crafting Skills utilizing gathering points typically require a tool kit to use during a preparation round. If the tool kit was purchased for a specific Skill, such as a climbing kit, then the character receives a Bonus to any Fate Rolls made while using their toolkit.

Special: Rogues begin the game with a Rogue Kit, which contains everything they need for pickpocketing, lock picking, and minor burglaries.

Starting Equipment:

Each class's starting equipment is listed under the class description. However, as an optional ruling, the Narrator may give the characters additional equipment and items to begin the game.

Using this option, characters may choose one of the following to begin the game with:
- 5 basic equipment level items
- 3 specialized equipment level items
- 1 artisan equipment level item

Players should discuss with their Narrator the specifics of the items they wish to start the game with. Using this rule can allow characters to work important items into their backstory, or increase the starting power level of your game.

In addition, characters beginning the game with a Tool Kit may exchange it for a different kit at the Narrator's discretion.

Crafting

Creating new items and equipment for your party can be a useful way to spend your preparation rounds. To create new items and equipment with Crafting Skills, characters must spend the Gathering Points they have accumulated.

Similar to how Money Points represent any valuable items the party has, Gathering Points (GP) represent raw materials used in the creation of new items. Gathering Points are generic, and a player may use their single pool of GP for different Crafting Skills. Finding Gathering Points (GP) is covered in further detail in **Chapter 6.**

Crafting Skills require a specialized tool kit to be effectively used. To craft a new item, first you must make any successful Skill Checks with the Craft's reliant abilities (detailed in **Chapter 11**). On a success, you may spend any amount of GP you possess in the creation of the item. Typically, crafted items cost *half* as many Gather Points as they would cost money points.

While any character may attempt to craft basic equipment without the proper training, more advanced tools and supplies require a more highly trained craftsperson. For each improved level of a Crafting Skill you possess, you may craft 1 higher level of equipment with that Skill.

While certain Crafting Skills, such as *Alchemy* and *Blacksmithing*, are detailed in **Chapter 11,** they do not represent the limit of your characters' crafting abilities. If you wish to be able to craft a specific set of tools or supplies not already outlined, discuss it with your Narrator to determine what reliant abilities would suit the Skill. For further information on creating new Skills see **Chapter 10.**

Magical Items

In worlds full of magic and wonder, magical items are powerful tools your characters can use throughout their journeys. Giving your characters unique magical items that suit their character and abilities can make for very compelling story rewards and create unique narrative moments.

Magical items can be enchanted with either Skills or Spells, granting characters access to abilities they normally wouldn't have. When creating a magical item for your characters, we recommend following the guidelines below:

Permanent Enchantments:

Effect	Score
Access to a Skill	+1 / level of Skill
Access to a Spell/Prayer, 1/day	+1 / each Spell level
Additional uses of a Spell/Prayer per day	+1 / Spell level for each additional usage
Single-use (potion or scroll)	-2 points

Equipment Level	Total Score
Artisan	1-7
Wondrous	7-15
Unique	15+

Example: During a Preparation round, our Mage wants to purchase a Wand that allows them to use the 3rd level Pyromancy 2 Spell 3/day. We could find the cost for this item by consulting the tables above:
- +3 for the 3rd level Spell
- +(2 X 3) = 6 for the 2 additional uses each day.
- Total Score: 9

This means the Equipment Level for this Wand would be Wondrous, and it would cost our player between 25,000 and 100,000 MP. Because 9 is towards the middle of the range for Wondrous items, you can set the final price towards the middle of the range as well, so this wand might cost around 60,000 MP).

Remember: If a character would like to craft the items instead of purchasing it, it should cost around half as much GP as it would MP.

STARFACE

Chapter 6: Preparation Rounds

Adventuring is no easy task. Whether your party is fighting against the forces or evil, or trekking out into the unknown, it's always good to be prepared for the journey ahead.

Preparation rounds represent periods of downtime and relative safety your party may experience. They typically take between 3 and 4 hours of in-game time and present your characters with opportunities to learn new Skills, gather supplies, and deepen their bonds as a group.

Preparation rounds typically occur at the beginning of a new day, while your party is traveling from one location to another, or when your party searches a new city for items and supplies[9].

During a preparation round, each character may take one action selected off of the list below:

- Train in 1 new Skill or Spell
- Try to improve a Skill you already possess
- Search for Gathering Points to use in the crafting of new items
- Attempt to Craft a new item or piece of equipment
- Gather information or research a specific topic
- Interact with nearby NPCs or shop for new equipment *without* using their action

Several of these actions are described in other chapters of the book. For information about training or improving Skills, see **Chapter 10.** For information about learning new Spells, see **Chapter 12.** For information about Crafting new items, see **Chapter 5.** The other options for preparation round actions are described in further detail throughout the rest of this chapter.

Gathering Points

To search for Gathering Points during a preparation round, make an Intelligence and a Wisdom Skill Check. On a success, roll a d100 and gain ten times that amount of GP.

Your preparation round doesn't go to waste on a failed Skill Check, however. You still roll a d100 but only gain an amount of GP equal to your roll. On an outcome of one success, one failure, you recieve five times the amount of your roll in GP.

Players are also not generally restricted from searching for gathering points due to their environment. However, if you'd like to add an increased level of realism to your game, you may change these rules to suit your game and play style.

If you wish as the Narrator, you may reward players with Bonuses for using Gathering Points in creative or interesting ways.

For example: if a character collects GP from a nearby forest enchanted with healing magic and uses them to craft a healing potion, you may decide that potion is more potent than an ordinary one and restores a greater amount of HP when consumed.

---

[9] I mean, who doesn't love a good shopping episode?

Researching and Finding Information

Occasionally it may be necessary for your characters to search for new information to aid in their quest. Whether searching through the great libraries of some larger cities or scouring through old tomes and stacks of notes, you never know when you'll find just the piece of information you need.

When searching for new information during a preparation round, you will typically make an Intelligence Skill Check for information gathered from books and academic sources, or a Charisma Skill Check to see what information you can gain from talking with local people nearby.

Upon a success, make a Fate Roll. The Narrator then describes any new information the character receives depending on the outcome.

For Example: Let's say our party is researching an ancient doomsday prophecy. They succeed they Skill Check, which means they have successfully found some piece of information about the prophecy. On an exceptionally high Fate Roll, they may discover a way to prevent the doomsday from occurring, while on a low Fate Roll they may realize the doomsday is happening much sooner than they thought.

On a failed Skill Check, the character should still make some progress towards learning new information, though what they learn may be hearsay or lead to further questions.

While the temptation exists to give your characters false information on a failed Skill Check here, this should be avoided. It's never satisfying for a party to invest their time in a game only to discover the thread they were chasing leads to a dead end.

Researching new topics is also a great way to allow players to explore facets of the world that aren't covered in this book. Rather than telling a player "No, that's not in this system," it becomes a practice of working together to create something new.

Allowing characters to invest their in-game time researching a brand new Spell or unlocking a long-hidden secret power can deepen your players' immersion in the game and make the world feel alive and full of mysteries to explore.

Strengthening Bonds

Preparation rounds also offer your party the opportunity to strengthen their bonds of friendship by role-playing together in character.

While some tables may be less interested in lengthy sections or role-playing conversations and want to spend more time on exploration and combat, other groups may find themselves devoting entire sessions to having conversations with the other characters.
(Note: This is a topic your group should consider covering during Session 0)

As the Narrator, you should encourage the characters to interact with each other and the world around them. Simple interactions between characters can easily lead to an increased sense of unity among the party members.

Chapter 7: Exploration Rounds

Whether your party is adventuring through dangerous wildernesses or delving into dungeons full of traps, exploration rounds represent those periods of time where your party is exploring their surroundings in an attempt to achieve their goals. While not under direct attack from an enemy, characters may still face dangers and challenges inherent to their surroundings.

A full exploration round lasts for about 30 minutes to 1 hour of in-game time, while an exploration encounter represents a short period of high-stress time for the party, similar to a combat encounter.

Similar to preparation rounds, each character may take 1 action during an exploration round. During this time, players may use any exploration Skills they have to learn about their environment or try to find a safe path forward.

While an exploration round is too short a period to attempt to craft new items or train new Skills, players who do not want to take an exploration action may attempt to leverage the other Skills they have at their disposal to assist their party.

The remainder of this chapter contains advice on building environments, running environmental encounters, and options for dealing with social encounters as well.

Creating Rich Environments

Exploration rounds give you as the Narrator an opportunity to tell the story through the environment the party is traveling through. Environmental storytelling can be a great way to draw your characters into the story and present obstacles they can't simply fight their way through.

This history of a location also provides you an opportunity to give the party hints or to foreshadow what obstacles might lie ahead.

More Than Sight
When building a new environment for your characters to explore, it's important to include other sensory details than just what your characters can see. While setting the scene for your characters, consider the following:

- What are the natural sounds of this area? If the characters stand still and listen, what could they hear?
- What is the air temperature? Is it cold or hot? Humid or arid?
- What does it *feel* like to travel through this place? Do branches cling to the characters as they pass? Does thick mud suck down on their boots?
- What smells exist here? What smells exist here that normally should not? Is there a sweet scent drifting through a battlefield, or the smell of death in a meadow of flowers?
- Is there anything visually striking about their environment? Anything out of the ordinary that would immediately catch the characters' attention.

It isn't necessary to describe every sense for every single environment your characters enter, but including a few extra details can help make your world seem that much more real to the other players.

"Random" Encounters

Random encounters and wandering monsters are a staple of many TTRPG experiences. But rather than let these encounters remain as non-sequiturs from your narrative, consider using them to build in further details and mysteries to your world.

An encounter with a wandering creature can be a great way to show your characters the types of creatures inhabiting this area, or better yet if the party can witness how the wildlife of your world interacts with each other. While an angry monster can certainly pose a true threat to a party, these encounters do not always have to be dangerous in order to impact how your party views the world around them.

An encounter with something out of the ordinary can also provide your characters with a great story hook to follow up on. If an aquatic monster appears in the middle of a desert, that's a natural mystery your party might be pulled towards investigating, and a future story waiting to be told!

Exploration Encounters

Exploration encounters are encounters where your party is dealing with threats from the environment itself rather than enemies fighting against them. Exploration encounters may include a trapped room deep within a dungeon, a rickety wooden bridge spanning a chasm, or even a chase through busy city streets.

Similar to combat encounters, exploration encounters represent a shorter period of high tension and stress where time slows down. Characters generally may not use preparation Skills during an exploration encounter, and at the Narrator's discretion may be unable to use certain exploration Skills depending on how much time and focus they require.

Instead of operating individual enemies as they would during a combat encounter, the Narrator instead operates the environmental threat the party must overcome.

Social Encounters

While not confined to exploration rounds, social encounters with NPCs share more in common with exploration encounters than with combat encounters[10].

Social encounters pose an obstacle to your party in the form of other non-player characters in the world. While these NPCs may not always be diametrically opposed to the party, oftentimes they must be convinced to offer their aid or assistance.

In other situations, the party may be talking to a political holdout to try and convince them to become an ally, or even talking down one of their enemies into no longer fighting. Social encounters allow your party another way to explore solving problems and overcoming obstacles.

Similar to exploration encounters, during a social encounter each character should have an opportunity to use any Skills or abilities they have to achieve their goal. You may use any of the methods for handling exploration encounters to handle social encounters too. Giving your NPCs 1 or 2 social Skills can help make the encounter more difficult for your players.

---

[10] Looking at you, murder hobos

Although you may use any method you like for tracking the attitudes and feelings of NPCs towards the party, presented below are two options within the framework of the NU and the Skill Check and Fate Roll system.

Percentage System

It can be easy to think of an NPC's Attitude towards the party as a percentage of how much the NPC likes or trusts the party. You can follow the table below for a guideline, but are free to adapt it to suit your game and play style.

Percentage (1-100)	Attitude
1-10	Hated enemy
11-25	Bitter rival, sever mistrust
25-33	Dislike, untrusting, suspicious
34-45	Cautious, wary
45-65	Polite, cordial, acquaintances
65-75	Friendly, familiar
76-89	Trusted friends, allies
90-100	Like family

Most NPCs will start towards the middle of the table and proceed outwards one way or another depending on the actions of the party. Though you can always roll a d100 to determine the starting Attitude of an NPC.

(Note: Adjusting the starting Attitudes of NPCs can easily help you set the tone of a new environment for the characters. In their hometown everyone may greet them warmly and kindly, increasing their starting Attitude.)

To determine the impact of the party's actions on an NPC, roll a d10 after any Skill Check is made, and increase their Attitude by that amount on a success, or lower it on a failure. The Narrator can always grant a Bonus or Penalty to this roll depending on how the players have role-played the situation.

Rather than start a fight, many NPCs will instead choose to stop interacting with the party and walk away if they reach a certain threshold, typically in the 25-33 range. Even if an NPC is pushed to the extreme lows, they may not be outwardly hostile or attack the party on sight[11].

Important social encounters may play out over several rounds of the characters attempting to sway the opinion of an NPC. Make sure to keep track of repeated successes and failures. Multiple successes in a row may start to build momentum in the party's favor, while multiple failures might cause the NPC to grow frustrated and stop interacting with the party even if they're an ally.

Incremental System

Rather than assigning a number range to each Attitude, instead we can just focus on the right-hand column of the table above and think of each row as an increment in the system.

Using this system, after a character makes a successful Skill Check during a social encounter, make a Fate Roll. On a positive

---

[11] There are many ways your party's enemies can work against them

outcome, move the NPC's Attitude up one or more steps. On a negative outcome, lower it instead.

This reduces the amount of math and numbers you need to keep track of as the Narrator, but may result in faster swings of an NPC's Attitude. A very high or low Fate Roll can turn a story-long enemy of the party into an ally, or if your party is unlucky turn a trusted ally into a new nemesis.

Bobo

Chapter 8: Combat Rounds

Whether fighting is your party's first or last option, most parties inevitably find themselves at odds with dangerous opponents. Combat encounters can add a thrilling element to your games and allow your characters to test their mettle in battle.

Reminder: You should always discuss how much combat you and your party want in the game during Session 0, as well as any limits to descriptions of violence.

Basic Combat Rules

Combat in the NU can be broken down into the following parts:
- Combat Order
- Action
- Damage
- Enemy Round

Combat Order
At the beginning of combat, each combatant rolls a d20, adding any bonus from the *Combat Readiness* Skill. Whoever rolls the highest overall wins the first action for their side. If there are more than 2 opposing sides involved in a combat encounter, whoever rolled second highest of the remaining sides wins the second action, so on and so forth. Each side then acts together as a group, in the order of how they rolled.

Action
During each round of an encounter, combatants may perform 1 action on each of their turns chosen from the list below[12]:
- Make an attack
- Use a Skill
- Defend yourself
- Cast a Spell
- Reposition
- Take Cover
- Prepare a contingent action

Make an attack: Characters may use their action to attack an enemy with their weapon. To do so, make a Skill Check using your character's Offense Rating. On a success, you deal damage to the target unless they can avoid your attack.

Use a Skill: Skills may be used in a variety of ways to gain the upper hand in battle, from attacking your enemies to bolstering your allies. You may use 1 Skill during each round with the Offensive, Defensive, or Utility action type.
- Offensive: Skills with offensive type actions modify or replace the normal attack your character can make. These are often more powerful attacks your characters can use a limited number of times.
- Defensive: When you are the target of an attack or Spell, you may attempt to avoid any damage that would be dealt to you by using a Defensive skill. These Skill Checks are made in the moment and take up the action of your *next* round of combat.
- Utility: These Skills can grant you a number of unique abilities in battle, especially with a little creativity. Certain Utility Skills may also allow you to use an Offensive Skill during the same turn.

---

[12] Beginning at level 10, characters may take 2 actions per round.

Defend Yourself: Even if you do not have a Defensive Skill to use, you may attempt to defend yourself with your action. Instead of a Skill Check, roll a d100 and reduce the amount of damage you take by that percentage. You still give up your next turn's action when defending an attack this way.

Cast a spell: Spellcasting classes may use their action to cast 1 Spell on their turn instead of using a Skill.

Reposition: If you are caught out of position or need to find a better angle, you may spend your action to safely move yourself around the battlefield.

Take Cover: You may use this action only provided there is enough cover to hide behind. While taking cover, you may not be directly targeted by any enemy attacks or spells. Taking an Offensive action or using certain Skills may expose you from your cover.

Prepare a Contingent Action: Instead of taking an action on your turn, you may instead prepare a specific action to be triggered by an event. You must select which Skill or Spell you would like to prepare as your contingent action ahead of time, as well as the specific trigger of your action. If the trigger does not occur before the end of the round, you may choose to use the contingent action then before the beginning of the next round.

Finishing the Round
If you make a successful attack and your opponent fails to defend against it, you deal damage to them. Methods for determining damage are covered in the next section.

After each member of the first side has had a chance to take an action on their turn, it is the opponent's turn. Any remaining opponents get a chance to take an action, provided they didn't use it to defend against an attack. Combat continues until all opponents are defeated or flee.

Determining Damage

There are several options for determining the damage of attacks and Spells. You should discuss these options with your group during Session 0 and pick one that best suits your game and play style.

Fate Roll Percentage
Whenever you deal damage to an enemy, make a Fate Roll. Take the result, including any Bonuses or Penalties applied by the Narrator, and deal an amount of damage equal to that percent of the target's total HP.

This method is straightforward and allows for dynamic swings in combat, but requires some math to be done by the players.

For encounters against very strong or evenly matched enemies, you may place a flat modifier on any damage Fate Rolls. If a party's attacks consistently fail to damage their enemy, this can be a good sign they are outmatched in the fight. Similarly, if both the party's and the opponent's attacks barely manage to land and deal damage, this can help the enemies feel like worthy opponents, matching your party's skill.

Storytelling Damage
Whenever you deal damage to an enemy, make a Fate Roll to determine how effective the attack was, adding any Bonuses or subtracting any Penalties applied to the

attack. Consult the table below to determine the level of damage dealt.

Fate Roll result	Damage level
1-10	Glancing
11-25	Superficial
26-40	Cutting
41-60	Injuring
61-80	Wounding
81-95	Breaking
95-100	Devastating

- Glancing: A light blow dealing little to no lasting damage
- Superficial: Cuts and bruises able to heal on their own in a short period of time
- Cutting: Deeper, bleeding cuts that can wear on an opponent
- Injuring: A solid hit dealing a significant amount of damage
- Wounding: An attack that leaves your opponent wounded, imposing a Penalty on the battlefield.
- Breaking: Wounds needing time or extra assistance outside of battle to heal properly
- Devastating: Opponent is knocked out of combat and left with a permanent penalty from the attack.

This method allows for your Narrator to use a wide variety of narrative consequences throughout combat, but does require more work on their behalf to determine the specific affects of each attack.

Damage Dice
If your group prefers a more traditional TTRPG experience of determining damage, your Narrator can set the damage dice of individual weapons and Spells. In this case, whenever you deal damage you roll your weapon or Spell's damage dice to determine how much damage you deal with each attack.

This system can make combat much more tactical and strategic but requires some work from the group to develop damage dice that suit each weapon as well as your game and play style.

Alternative: For parties looking for a more difficult combat experience, when reduced to 0 hp characters may die instead, needing to be revived by a powerful healer or replaced by a new character altogether. You should discuss the level of deadliness your characters will face during Session 0.

Reaching 0 Health Points

The following section contains discussion of character death and dying.

When a combatant is reduced to 0 HP, they are incapacitated and removed from the battle unless they can be revived by their allies, either through magic or healing skills. Characters still incapacitated at the end of combat must spend their next preparation round recovering from their injuries before they return to full health. The Narrator may also impose permanent in-game impairment until they are able to be fully restored by a powerful healer.

In some games, you may decide you want your characters to face more lethal dangers. As an alternative to falling unconscious, your characters may die when they reach 0 HP, needing to be resurrected by magic or replaced with a new character.

Especially damaging attacks may knock your characters unconscious, or worse, before they reach 0 HP. If you're using the Storytelling damage option presented above, certain Breaking and most Devestating attacks may be enough to remove a combatant from the encounter.

You should discuss the level of mortal danger you want your characters to be placed in during Session 0.

Iron Waffles, Rival of Baconface Omega

Chapter 9: Narrating the Game

The Narrator is the player in the game who, well, narrates the story for the rest of the players in the game. While they do take on some extra responsibilities in this role, it is important to remember the Narrator is a player at the table just like the others and should enjoy the experience just the same.

Rather than playing the main character or acting as an omnipotent adversary to the party, Narrators are encouraged to tell a story alongside the other players at the table. A Fate Roll may change the game at a moment's notice, so Narrators are unable to control exactly where the story goes.

Instead, as a Narrator you should rely on your knowledge of the world you've created, as well as engaging with the other players at the table to tell dramatic, compelling stories with your friends.

This chapter contains advice on how to narrate a game within the Narrative Universe, including how to interpret and modify Fate Rolls, build a rich world for the other players to explore, and handle mechanics on the fly.

Session 0

As with any TTRPG, the stories you can tell within the NU vary greatly in tone and style. Not every player enjoys gritty, realistic games. Some groups may prefer less violence at the table, or even no direct combat at all. Remember Rule #1: There is no wrong way to play the game, so long as everyone at your table is having fun.

It is the responsibility of not just the Narrator, *but every player at the table* to help ensure everyone else is having a good time.

As the Narrator, however, you are often the player left in charge of organizing a game and building the initial setting and story for the characters. To that end, holding an initial Session 0 before officially beginning your campaign can greatly benefit you throughout the entire story. Session 0 also offers the other players a chance to meet and discuss their characters. Topics to include in your Session 0 are:

Tone: The overall feeling or mood of your game. Will you be telling the story of a dark, dramatic mystery, a high epic fantasy, or a light-hearted adventure?

Setting[13]**:** When and where is the story taking place? What is the world of the story like? How did the characters all arrive at the location where the story will begin?

Characters: Session 0 is a great opportunity for players to discuss what characters they're thinking of playing. This helps ensure everyone is happy with their choices and the party will be able to work together once the game begins. Players can also build their characters together during Session 0 if everyone likes!

Combat/Roleplay Mix: While some groups may hardly spend any time having conversations with each other in character, others will spend entire sessions exploring the personal world of their characters. You

---

[13] While this manual focuses on fantasy themed games, the NU rules are easily adaptable to any setting! Feel free to re-flavor magical abilities as sci-fi tech if that suits your game better.

should discuss how much combat and exploration you want in your game vs how much time you would like to spend roleplaying.

Safety Tools: It's important to know what *not* to include in your games. Establishing clear lines of communication between players helps ensure the game remains fun for everyone. *Appendix A* contains a sample consent form for you to use with your group to start this conversation. You should also have a way for players to inform you when they are feeling uncomfortable in a scene and need it to move on.

Session 0 also allows you as the Narrorator to learn about the characters and their backstories. Tying in elements of the story to your characters' backstories not only makes for compelling, interesting stories but helps the other players feel like a larger part of the narrative.

Even though aspects of the story may change suddenly with a Fate Roll, you can begin to build the larger framework for your campaign based on details from the conversation with your players, and their characters' backstories.

To include the other players even more in developing the campaign, you can ask for their input in creating details about the world and setting.

Writing Prompt[14]: During Session 0, ask each player to create 1 fact about the world and 1 rumor that local townspeople are talking about. This is a great way to generate details about your world and story hooks for your characters to investigate.

------

[14] More prompts are available in **Appendix D**

Session 0 should be an enjoyable experience where the players can get together and begin getting invested in their characters and the story you will all be telling together.

Building your World

As the Narrator, you are in charge of describing the surroundings of the players, the action that occurs in the game, and portraying any Non-Player Characters (NPCs) the other players meet throughout the story.

Having a well-defined idea of the world, its people, and the events within it will not only help you in narrating the game but also in adjusting the story to the outcome of any Fate Rolls that might suddenly change it.

Hopefully, you have received some feedback or details from your players during Session 0 to help you begin to build your world. It is often best to start small, with a single town or city, and expand outwards as your characters naturally explore the world.

While some Narrators may enjoy creating finely detailed worlds for their characters to explore, others may leave many of the details blank, allowing for the other players at the table to fill in much of the history and events of the world. Neither is inherently better or worse, it just depends on what helps the players at your table feel immersed in the world and the story.

There are a few things you will want to be sure to include in any worldbuilding you do. If there are people, places, or organizations important to a character's backstory, be sure to include them in your world. These can be excellent places to start looking for plot hooks to draw your players into the story.

It's also important to know about the location your characters will be starting in as this will alter the story greatly. Is the party beginning in a large city or a small town? What sort of people live in this area? What problems do they have the party may be able to help with?

Worldbuilding is also a great place to focus your efforts on preparing for your next session. As the story progresses, knowing about your world and the character's surroundings can help you adjust the narrative as you play. A Fate Roll can add dramatic threats or wondrous events to the story at any time. A good knowledge of the world can help you make sure those events make sense within the larger story.

Providing your party with details about the world around them can greatly enhance your storytelling, providing your narratives with depth and richness, and helping the other players get invested in the story.

For more ideas about worldbuilding, as well as questions and prompts to help you get started, see **Appendix D**.

Story Hooks

Whether you're just beginning your journey, or your characters have just completed their most recent quest, the Narrator will present the party with story hooks to lead them in the direction of interesting plot lines and decisions they must make.

A "story hook" is a detail designed to grab the party's attention and get them invested in the narrative. Story hooks can be anything from a "Help Wanted" poster in the local tavern, to a rumor whispered to a character from a passerby.

At the beginning of your campaign, it may be necessary to provide your party with a number of different story hooks to discover what your characters are most interested in pursuing.

Hopefully, you have a good place to start with these early story hooks from Session 0. Connecting early story elements to the characters' backstories is a great way to get your party invested and interested in the story.

You can also look for story hooks within your worldbuilding. What events are happening in the area to draw the party's attention? Who might need the party's help with a task? What clues have the party's adversaries left behind, leading the party into a new mystery?

It's important not to force a particular story hook on a party not interested in pursuing it. Instead, focus on the aspects of the narrative the other players are invested in and eager to explore more. Not only will this lead to a better story, but also a more enjoyable game for all involved.

Stakes and Obstacles

What makes a story most interesting for both the characters and Narrator is the party being in situations where they are forced to make difficult decisions. Utilizing stakes and obstacles as a Narrator will help you to do so.
The "stakes" of a situation represent what is at risk for the characters, the bad thing that will happen if they fail to achieve their goal.

Simply put, it means what is at stake for the party?

Obstacles are anything that gets in the way of the party achieving their goals. This can be adversaries fighting against them, the environment posing a threat, or even personal conflict within the party itself.

As a storyteller, it is important to remember these concepts as you are playing the game. A story without any real stakes for the players can quickly lose focus and interest, while a story without any true obstacles for the party isn't as dramatic or exciting.

Playing the Villain

As the Narrator, one of your jobs at the table is to portray any villains or adversaries the party comes across. A compelling or even sympathetic villain can add a great dynamic to your games, and introduce plenty of drama to your narrative.

Stories need to have obstacles and villains for their heroes to overcome, but it's important not to get too caught up in your role as the adversary. The NU is a collaborative storytelling game, and your goal should always be to tell a story with the other players at the table, and not to *beat* them at the game.

There are many ways to play a compelling villain that don't include heinous acts. Avoid going for the shock value of these, especially when it may conflict with a player's preferences discussed during Session 0. Villains are more interesting to the story when they provide a moral dilemma for the characters.

(*Note:* Some tables may prefer a more adversarial Narrator, and should discuss this during Session 0)

Interpreting Fate Rolls

Perhaps the most important responsibility of the Narrator is being the player to interpret the results of Fate Rolls. A particularly high or low Fate Roll can dramatically change the path of your story, and being able to adapt to these changes is a key skill Narrators must develop.

Fate Rolls are made using a 100-sided die, giving Narrators a larger spectrum of possible results. This allows you to add a great deal of nuance to the outcome of a Fate Roll, adding in shades of good luck and lurking threats to your narration.

You may use the table on the following page as a base guide for interpreting the results of Fate Rolls. As always, feel free to adjust this based on what suits your game and play-style.

Brain-O, the Over Brain

Result	Impact
1	Catastrophic impact on the party and game
2-10	"Worst case scenario" outcomes
11-25	Very bad outcome, little to no positive
26-40	Poor outcome, presents a difficult path ahead
41-59	Mixed outcome, party may get what they want but at a cost
60-74	Positive outcome for the party but with some setback or difficulty
75-89	Very good outcome for the party, nearly all positive
90-99	"Best case scenario" outcomes
100	Deus-ex-machina like outcome for the party

Fate Rolls should be made as a result of the party's actions, and present new choices the party must make. No matter the result of the Fate Roll, the story should progress forward. There should never be a moment in your game when a player makes a Fate Roll and nothing happens. As Narrator, try to put your characters in situations where they are forced to make difficult choices. Those choices lead to characters taking actions, leading back to another round of Skill Checks and Fate Rolls to keep the story moving forward.

Example: Your party is attempting to break into a villain's castle to thwart an evil plan. Let's say they've failed their initial Skill Check to climb the walls. As the Narrator, you make a Fate Roll with a high outcome. Even though the party has failed their check to climb to the top of the wall, perhaps in their attempt they reached an open window and found their way into an empty room.

Once inside, your party attempts to sneak around the castle undetected. This time, they succeed their Skill Check, but you make a low Fate Roll afterwards. Here, they may move around the castle undetected, but discover the villain's plan is much further along than they anticipated. This forces the party to make a choice: do they still attempt to stop the villain now and face an increased threat, or do they risk the villain's plan coming further into fruition by leaving to get reinforcements?

Whether the outcome of the Fate Roll is good or bad for the party, try to tie the outcome into natural consequences of the action. This can help you determine what happens more quickly and keep your game grounded. It is possible for a skilled Narrator to run an entire game in the NU without preparing the story ahead of time, while simply relying on Fate Rolls and the other players at the table to help lead the way.

As your characters become more powerful, they are capable of achieving greater feats, and this should reflect in the outcomes of your Fate Rolls. You can scale Fate Rolls to whatever power level the party is currently at. A party of demi-gods might regularly change the shape of reality, but for a group playing all babies, a 100 on a Fate Roll might mean they stand up on their own 2 feet and walk across the room.[15]

Modifying Fate Rolls

There are many situations where characters may tilt the balance of fate one way or another. As the Narrator, whenever you feel appropriate you may grant a Bonus or a Penalty to a Fate Roll depending on the situation.

If the characters have made a series of smart choices and have gained an advantage, then it is appropriate to grant a Bonus to a Fate Roll to reward their hard work. On the other hand, if a character wants to attempt a risky maneuver that could easily end in disaster, those circumstances may warrant a Penalty to the roll.

Throughout this book, the generic terms "Bonus" and "Penalty" are applied to any effects that modify Fate Rolls and Skill Checks. Many skills, for example, grant characters a Bonus on Fate Rolls with a successful Skill Check.

This section presents several options for handling Bonuses and Penalties depending on how difficult the party enjoys their game, and how much math you want to do at your table.

Remember: As with any optional ruling, you should discuss the alternatives with your group during Session 0 to determine which method works best for your game.

____

[15] Yes, babes. I *said* any characters and I meant it, dammit.

Numbered Bonuses and Penalties
A more traditional way to modify Fate Rolls, numerical Bonuses and Penalties can be added or subtracted from the outcome of a Fate Roll. As a general guideline, we recommend starting with adding or subtracting 5 from the result of a Fate Roll for each Bonus or Penalty.

For example: If a character attempting to talk an enemy out of fighting succeeds on their Skill Check to do so, they would be given +5 to their Fate Roll to determine how much they have swayed the enemy's Attitude.

Bonuses and Penalties can also stack with each other. So in the situation above, if the character attempted to use 2 Skills instead of just 1, and succeeded on both of the Skill Checks, they would be given a +10 instead.

It is easy to keep track of Bonuses and Penalties this way, even if the situation gets complex.

For example: Let's say the party is trying to talk down an aggressive opponent like in the situation above. If the opponent has reason not to trust the party, the party may receive a Penalty to their Fate Roll. If the same character still succeeds on both of their Skill Checks, we can break down the Bonuses and Penalties in the following way:
- +5 Bonus for the first Skill Check
- +5 Bonus for the second Skill Check
- -5 Penalty for the opponent's mistrust

The player would be awarded a total of +5 to the total of their Fate Roll in this example.

In some cases, it may become necessary to limit the total number of Bonuses your characters can stack onto a single Fate

Roll. Especially as characters accumulate more Skills at higher levels, the potential exists to slow down your game considerably by continually searching for more Bonuses with the "perfect" combination of Skills.[16]

In most cases, we recommend a limit of 2 to 3 Skills be used for any Fate Roll from a single character. If multiple characters are working together in a Group Skill Check, limit each to 1 or 2 Skills depending on how many characters are involved.

Adjusting the base number of 5 up or down can easily affect how difficult the game feels for your players. Lowering the Bonuses and Penalties and leaving the results of Fate Rolls more up to chance can make for a more challenging game while increasing Bonuses and Penalties allows players to take more direct control of their rolls.

As the Narrator, it is up to you to determine the exact amount for each Bonus or Penalty to be applied. You should base this decision on the conversation you had with your players during Session 0.

Favorable & Unfavorable Fate Roll
The simplest way to modify Fate Rolls is to turn them into Favorable Fate Rolls with a Bonus, and Unfavorable Fate Rolls with a Penalty. Instead of the normal spectrum of outcomes detailed earlier in this chapter, Favorable and Unfavorable Fate Rolls tilt the balance highly towards either a good or a bad outcome.

This method of modifying Fate Rolls can lead to dramatic moments in your game and requires less math to be done at your table.

You may use the tables below as a guideline for determining the outcome of Fate Rolls made under favorable or unfavorable circumstances.

Favorable Fate Roll Table:

Result	Impact
1 - 10	Very bad outcome, little to no positive
11 - 33	Poor outcome, presents a difficult path ahead
34 - 50	Mixed outcome, party may get what they want but at a cost
51 - 66	Positive outcome for the party but with some minor setback or difficulty
66 - 84	Very good outcome for the party, nearly all positive
85 - 99	"Best case scenario" outcomes
100	Deus-ex-machina like outcome for the party

---

[16] Hint: It does't exist

Unfavorable Fate Roll Table:

Result	Impact
100 - 91	Very good outcome for the party, nearly all positive
90 - 75	Mostly positive outcome with some cost or drawback
74 - 60	Mixed success, party may get what they want but at a cost
59 - 40	Poor outcome, presents a difficult path ahead
39 - 20	Very bad outcome, a clear danger or threat to the party
19 - 2	"Worse case scenario" outcomes
1	Catastrophic, campaign altering outcome

These tables are just a guideline and represent a balanced range of outcomes. As the Narrator, you can adjust these tables as you see fit, depending on how difficult the rest of the players enjoy their games.

Modifying Skill Checks

Certain Skills and Equipment grant characters a Bonus to their Skill Checks. A simple way to handle these Bonuses is to increase the Character's effective Ability score by 2 for the purposes of determining the outcome of the Skill Check.

For Example: Let's say the party is exploring ancient, lost ruins. One of the party members would like to use their *Archeology* Skill to see if they can learn about the location. They have a Toolkit for *Arhceology* and are using it for the Skill Check. *Archeology* has a Reliant Ability of Intelligence, and our character's Intelligence score is 12. When they roll their Skill Check, they would act as if their Intelligence score was 14 to determine if it was successful.

As the Narrator, you may also grant situational Bonuses to Skill Checks as you see fit. These don't always have to be an adjustment to the character's Ability score, and can be any effect you feel suits the circumstances.

Mixed Success

Mixed successes generally result in the character getting something they want but at a cost or consequence. They are a fantastic way to keep your story moving forward while putting your characters in situations where they must make interesting decisions. A mixed success generally results from a Fate Roll outcome towards the middle of its range.

You can rely on the situation the characters are in, including the environment and any nearby NPCS, to determine the outcome of a Mixed Success.

Example: Let's take our previous example of a party attempting to infiltrate a villain's castle[17]. They have succeeded their Skill Check to go unnoticed by the guards of the Castle, but this time their Fate Roll results in a Mixed Success. They should still have a path forward towards their goal, but with an added difficulty. Perhaps now they

---

[17] Found on Page 43

encounter a trap designed to detect any movement near an important location, or the villain has employed guards that rely on more than just their sight to detect the party.

Boons

Boons are an optional mechanic that allows Narrators to reward players for creative roleplay or exceptional character moments. Boons allow a player to ensure their Fate Roll has a positive outcome before rolling any dice. Boons may only be used once, and when used the minimum result of the Fate Roll they are used on becomes 60.

In game, Boons represent divine favors granted to the characters from deities and other powerful beings, allowing the characters to call upon them in a time of dire need.

Boons can additionally be used to ask these powerful beings for a larger favor. When used this way, the player gives up the ability to determine the outcome of a Fate Roll. In exchange, they may ask for a powerful favor from whatever being granted them the boon. Make a Fate Roll to determine the being's response.

Get creative in what beings grant Boons in your world. A Boon from a king or queen could grant the party elevated social status, while a Boon from a power Mage could give them a one-time use of a powerful spell.

Handling Mechanics

NU TTRPG Rule Zero: Skills are the narrative, the Narrator is the mechanics

In many cases it will be necessary for you as the Narrator to determine the mechanics of Skills and Spells in your game. As they are written in this manual, most Skills and Spells describe narrative options the characters have at their disposal rather than defined mechanics in game. The Skill list in **Chapter 11** provides you with the basic details of each Skill's mechanics, such as their Reliant Abilities. Certain details though, such as specific ranges or areas of effect, are left to your Narrator's discretion to determine how these abilities play out your game.

When making a judgment call regarding in-game mechanics, refer back to the questions presented in the **Narrator's Discretion** section in **Chapter 1** for advice. To summarize those questions here: Does it make sense within the narrative, does it tell a good story, and does it allow the players at the table to have fun?

Remember: Telling a good story does not always mean things go how the party wants them to. Do not be afraid to make a call that goes against the party if you feel the situation necessitates it. Stories need to feel grounded, with an internal sense of logic and rules for how the world operates. An ungrounded story quickly loses any real sense of urgency for what's at stake.

A good example of this principle is in the use of a character's Skills. While players should feel free to use their Skills in creative ways not explicitly listed in this manual, there should also be a limit to what they can accomplish with those Skills. A character trained in *Acrobatics* might be able to use their skills to parkour up a wall, but probably can't flip up to the same height in an open field.

As the Narrator, you can always use a Fate Roll to help determine the specific effects for Skills and Spells. If a Spell has an area of effect, you can use a Fate Roll to determine just how many enemies are caught in the spell.

The NU is an infinitely customizable system. By following the guidelines presented in this book, your group can create new systems and concepts for your characters to explore, such as new classes, Skills, Spells, and even power sources. Work together as a group to determine how these new powers function, or better yet, have characters within your games and stories work to discover these new powers!

Beginning Your Story

From peaceful country towns to raucous taverns, every adventure has to begin somewhere, but it can often be difficult to find a good place to start.

If this is your first time narrating a game in the NU, here is some advice to help you begin your story and navigate the different rounds in the game.

But First…We Prepare
Preparation rounds are a natural way to begin your sessions. This allows the characters a chance to prepare their Skills and discuss where they would like to go next[18].

Especially if this is the first session of a new campaign, Preparation rounds give your players a chance to introduce their characters to the others at the table and roleplay a little of the beginning of their day.

____

[18] It helps a lot if you pay attention to that part

Initial Hooks
After each character has had an opportunity to introduce themselves and prepare for the adventure ahead, introduce the party to your initial story hook. This should be a compelling reason to get all the party members together and working towards the same goal.

Finding an initial story hook that ties in aspects of each character's backstory can help your party unify around a single goal. Don't be afraid to discuss how your story will start with your players at Session 0 so everyone can help create a cohesive party.

If you're still struggling to find a good beginning for your story, answer the following question: What makes this day different than any other? Stories don't normally begin on ordinary days when nothing of any importance happens.

Onwards to Exploration
After your players are hooked into the initial story, you will most likely progress to an Exploration round. This allows the party to gather information about their surroundings and the quest at hand.

If you're in a city or urban environment, the party might be asking around for information or navigating busy city streets. In the wilderness, your party might be dealing with inclement weather or treacherous mountain passes.

Introducing Encounters
At some point, your party should face a situation that requires the use of their Skills to safely proceed. Encounters allow the Narrator to introduce obstacles that must be overcome and decisions that must be made.

Encounters can be based around the party's environment, NPCs they meet, or enemies they encounter. Remember though, encounters should move the story forward and force the party to make choices that will impact the game.

A Narrative Universe Classic
If you're still looking for a good place to begin your game, look no further than this NU classic!

After the party introduces themselves during an initial Preparation round, they receive a call for help from Granny Goodwin, a kindhearted woman in the local town.

You see, Granny Goodwin has a problem: there's a rat in her basement and she can't seem to get it out. She hires the party to come to her house and help fix this seemingly simple problem.

The rat, however, is never just a rat. Sometimes it's a monstrous rat. Sometimes is a supernatural force. Sometimes Granny Goodwin was luring the party into her basement to cook them into a soup… The choice is yours as Narrator but it always provides a fun basis for the rest of your adventure.

The following sections contain tools and systems you can use as the Narrator during Preparation, Exploration, and Combat rounds.

Party Interaction Prompts

Preparation rounds are the only rounds in the game dedicated to times when the party isn't in any direct threat or danger. While you should encourage roleplay throughout the game as the Narrator, preparation rounds give you an opportunity to place players in situations where they are forced to explore the personal side of their characters.

2 Truths and a Lie
While this classic ice-breaker game has been around for a long time, it can serve as a powerful tool to not only spark ideas for interactions between the characters of your party but also lets the players get to know their own character a little better too!

Before the game begins, have each player write down 2 truths and 1 lie about their character. Then, the Narrator will take the pieces of paper and randomly distribute them to other members of the party. Be sure a character does not receive their own truths or lie.

When complete, each player should have several potential truths or lies for the other characters in their party. They can use this information to start conversations with other party members, either sharing common ground or addressing a concerning rumor.

While interparty drama can make for dramatic moments in game, players need to remember that everything should stay in the world of the game and no one's feelings should get hurt for real. You should discuss party dynamics during Session 0.

On Watch Together
It is common for adventuring parties to have a member or two be on watch throughout their nights at camp. Introducing a small, non-threatening event during the evening, such as a small animal wandering into camp or one of the sleeping members snoring exceptionally loudly, can be a subtle way to

encourage those party members to interact with each other.

Dice Rolls

A more random method of placing characters in situations where they can role-play is to roll dice during a preparation round. Assign each character a number on a die. Then roll the die twice to determine which two characters are placed in an interaction together. You can come up with any kind of situation you like for this interaction, or if you prefer, you can roll a d10 and consult the table below.

Result	Situation
1	One of the characters needs help from the other
2	The two characters get into a disagreement
3	One of the characters confides something with the other
4	The two characters discover something new in camp
5	The two characters get lost during the preparation round
6	One of the characters tells the other a secret
7	The two characters notice something new about another party member
8	One of the characters tells the other a rumor they've heard
9	The two characters find themselves alone together
10	One of the characters confesses something to the other

Exploration Round Mechanics

Exploration encounters add drama and excitement to your game without having the party enter a violent conflict with opponents. As Narrator, you have mechanical discretion over how any traps or environmental threats operate in the game. Below are several options for you to use during environmental encounters. You can mix and match several of the options to add even more pressure to a situation.

Fate Rolls

The Narrator's primary tool, Fate Rolls are a fantastic way to handle exploration encounters. Simply allow the characters to attempt any Skill Checks they would like to overcome the threat or obstacle, and then make a Fate Roll with any Bonuses or Penalties from their Skill Check.

You can resolve the exploration encounter like you would any other Fate Roll, interpreting the results and narrating the action to your party. If this would result in damage being dealt to a character, refer to the **Determining Damage** section in **Chapter 8.** It may take characters several rounds of actions to successfully overcome an exploration encounter.

Ticking Clock

To add a great deal of pressure to your party for time-sensitive situations, you can add a running clock to the encounter - either by counting down a certain number of rounds or by introducing a literal running clock. The party should be aware time is of the essence in these situations. If they don't know there is a time limit, they won't feel any increased pressure.

If the party fails to pass the obstacle or achieve their goal within the time allowed, you should make a Fate Roll with some Penalty to determine the outcome.

(Note: To easily combine the ticking clock with Fate Rolls, at the end of each round make a Fate Roll to determine if anything happens. Every round, add another Penalty to the Fate Roll. This adds a level of unpredictability to your encounters!)

Using Skills and Spells

If you want to make the environment less passive, or your exploration encounter includes some traps to surprise the characters, include some Skills or Spells as abilities to use during the encounter.

Choose several Skills or Spells that make sense in the context of your encounter. If your party is scaling a mountain, consider Skills that might cause the party to slip or lose their grip. If your encounter has traps, consider using some Rogue Skills for extra impact. You can easily re-flavor any Spells or Skills to suit the encounter you've created.

It's a...

Traps can add a level of unpredictability and danger to your exploration rounds, but can also be frustrating for players to face sometimes. While hidden traps are popular in many modern media depictions, they can function better in your TTRPG game if the characters *know* where the trap is.

Rather than your traps punishing players for not inspecting an area closely enough, consider traps like an open-ended puzzle, similar to your combat encounters. Traps are a problem the party must solve with an obvious consequence if they fail. As with all solutions, you should allow your characters to get creative in how they approach and solve traps.

Sample Exploration Encounters

The following section contains sample encounters you can use in your games, or as a guideline to create your own.

The Rickety Bridge

While exploring, your characters discover an old rope bridge spanning a wide chasm. While they can climb down and attempt to find another way, that will take time and may prove to be even more dangerous. The bridge *may* be stable enough to cross, but there's no telling when it will give way. How will your party find their way across?

You can run the Rickety Bridge encounter using Fate Rolls and counting down rounds. Determine how many rounds it should take your party to reach the other side of the bridge unimpeded. Set this as the number of rounds after which the bridge will collapse.

At the end of each round your party is on the bridge, make a Fate Roll with a Penalty in secret. On any unfavorable result, take away 1 or more rounds from the countdown, reducing the total amount of time before the bridge collapses.

If your party takes precautions to reinforce the bridge or secure it to either side of the chasm, add 1 or more rounds to the countdown to represent the bridge having extra time before it falls.

Fate Rolls being made in secret here adds a level of suspense to the encounter as the party is never sure when the bridge will go. You should use descriptions as the Narrator to give the party hints about the bridge's condition - boards falling out from beneath their feet, sudden vibrations, the threads of the ropes slowly unwinding… these also help increase the feeling of urgency for the party members.

The Cursed Idol

Deep within an ancient crypt lies a tablet from a long-forgotten deity. Many have tried to claim this power for their own, and many have failed. Over the years the legend of the tablet's curse began to spread through the local towns, drawing many would-be adventurers to their deaths.

The Cursed Idol can serve as the final encounter of a dungeon your players are exploring. Upon entering the trapped chamber, the party sees an ancient tablet sitting on a pedestal in the middle of the room. Scattered all around the pedestal are bodies in various states, however, there is a clear ring around the pedestal where no one has fallen.

Upon closer inspection, the party may discover that the "curse" of the tablet is little more than an elaborate trap - the mechanism lies within the pedestal and the tablet itself is a part of it. When pulled from its resting place, a powerful magic spell is unleashed, knocking anyone nearby backward with devastating force. However, if pushed inward instead of pulled out, the tablet reveals the true treasure of the tomb…

Get creative with the solution of this trap if you feel your party is up for a more difficult challenge.

The Forgotten Place

While traveling through a dense forest, the party stumbles upon the ruins of a town long since lost to history. The forest has almost entirely reclaimed the forgotten town, with greenery growing up and through many of the old buildings. Moss covered walls lie half fallen, giving a glimpse into the inside of the buildings. Home, shops, temples, people use to *live* here…where did they go?

The Forgotten Place is an encounter that allows players to use their Skills to solve the mystery of this location, adding a level of depth and intrigue to your exploration round as your players search the ruins for clues.

You should have an idea of what happened to the town beforehand and include specific details that might help your players pick up on what happened. Maybe all the buildings are cleared of their belongings, hinting that the inhabitants simply picked up their things and left. Maybe there are clues about a mysterious sickness, or a dark force that was unleashed in the area. Feel free to adjust this reason if the party comes up in a theory they are all excited about and you feel fits the narrative of the game.

The Flooded Temple

The party is exploring an old island temple when the tide starts to come in unexpectedly, quickly flooding the building and forcing the players to scramble if they want to escape safely.

This encounter can be run similarly to a chase sequence, with the party trying to outrun the rising water levels instead of something pursuing them.

Allow the characters to use their Skills each round in an attempt to escape more quickly or gain ground on the rising water. At the end of the round, make a Fate Roll and add any Bonuses or Penalties from the characters' Skill Checks. On a favorable outcome, the party gets closer to the surface and escaping the island. Be sure to add some obstacles like a broken staircase or falling debris to challenge your players as they make their escape.

Should the temple flood before your party can escape, the encounter becomes a test of their Constitution to see if they can hold their breath long enough to make it back to the surface.

Sample Social Encounters

The following section contains sample social encounters you can use in your game, or as a guideline to create your own. These samples use the percentage system for social encounters.

The Stubborn Informant

While searching for information, the party finds someone who may be willing to talk…for the right price.

The informant has some valuable information regarding the party's current goal, but they need to be convinced in order to share it. Their starting Attitude towards the party is a 33, suspicious and wary. They are risking a lot by talking to the party, so any Fate Roll to improve their Attitude suffers a Penalty.

The informant will walk away from the party if their Attitude reaches a 25 or below, or if the party fails 3 Skill Checks in a row. To successfully get them to talk, the party must raise their Attitude to at least 50.

The party should leverage their social skills to try and improve the informant's Attitude. The party may attempt to bribe the informant, or otherwise gain their favor, in which case they no longer suffer a Penalty to their Fate Rolls. They can also try to use their environment to their advantage - buying the informant a drink if they're in a tavern can easily get them talking.

Wary Allies

While searching for allies to join their cause, your party has encountered 2 opposing factions. Each offers valuable assistance to the party if they were to join their alliance, but refuse to if the other will be involved. Can the party help negotiate an alliance between the two factions?

The Wary Allies encounter forces your party to balance the Attitudes of 2 different groups of NPCs with not only themselves, but each other. Each opposing side of the negotiations should begin with their Attitude towards the party at around 60, polite and cordial, and their attitude towards the *other* faction around 35, wary and mistrusting.

The party must use their Skills to help the factions Attitudes improve towards each other while not losing the trust of the factions themselves. The negotiators will walk away from discussions if their Attitude towards the party falls below 45, or their Attitude with the other side falls below 25. Both factions should make initial demands that are unacceptable to the other. The party must convince them to compromise on their demands without offending them. Make a Fate Roll at the end of each round of negotiations to determine how the 2 factions Attitude changes towards each other. Be sure to include any Bonuses your party gains from successful Skill Checks.

Exclusive Access

Your party needs to gain access to an elite social club in order to speak with one of its members who is a noble. The bouncer insists that a password is required, and refuses to let the party enter or speak to whoever is in charge. The party must find a way to deal with the stoic bouncer and get into the club if they don't want to loose their lead.

The bouncer should begin with their Attitude towards the party around 45, still cordial and polite as they are only doing their job. The party takes a Penalty to any Fate Rolls to improve the bouncer's Attitude as they are being paid well by the club not to let anyone in without a password.

They will not open the door for the party willingly unless their Attitude reaches 75. On the other hand, they will quickly shut the party out of the club if their Attitude drops any lower than 35.

The party may attempt to persuade the bouncer directly, or attempt to get them to reveal the password. In this encounter, your party may have better luck trying indirect tactics rather than trying to simply talk their way through.

A Desperate Bargain

This encounter sees your party attempting to talk down an enemy from a hostage situation, and may not be appropriate for all tables.

Towards the end of a combat encounter, when the enemy is sure to be defeated, the final combatant grabs an innocent passerby, holding them hostage unless the party allows them to go free. Their starting Attitude towards the party should be around 15 or lower since they were just in armed combat.

The party will suffer a Penalty to their Fate Rolls if they try to improve the enemy's Attitude directly, potentially putting the innocent person at greater risk. The party must use their Skills to attempt to deescalate the situation and find a peaceful solution. Alternatively, they may use their social Skills as a distraction, allowing another party member to get into a position where they can deal with the threat.

Unless you have specifically discussed this aspect of your game beforehand, the innocent hostage should remain unharmed throughout the encounter. The worst case scenario should be the enemy making a run for it rather than violence.

Designing Combat Encounters

Finding the right balance of challenge and fun in your combat encounters can be difficult for anyone running a TTRPG. Combat encounters need to feel like they pose a true threat to the party, otherwise the game and the story lose their stakes. On the other hand, players should feel rewarded for making smart decisions during battle and not like they are whittling away at a large bag of Health Points.

Combat as an "Open-Ended Puzzle"

Think of the combat encounters you create not as delicate balancing acts or tests in repetitive addition and subtraction, but as puzzles for your players to solve. The "pieces" are monsters, NPCs, the environment, and the characters' abilities. The solution can be anything narratively fulfilling and is fully up to your players' creativity! Out of the box thinking, roleplay, and interesting use of Skills should be rewarded with quick and beneficial resolutions to combat encounters.

For example: The party is facing off against a giant near a cliff-side. While fighting the giant head-on may prove deadly for the party, they may be able to use their environment to their advantage. Either through causing a rock-slide from above, or finding a way to push the giant off the edge of the cliff, they can find a creative solution to the encounter.

It is important in these cases the party understands the consequences of fighting their enemy head on. Consider having very powerful enemies show off their might before attacking the party, or show little response to the party's regular attacks to show the players the threat they are dealing with.

Note: This approach to designing combat encounters may not appeal as much to a group who enjoys more hack & slash combat. As the Narrator, you should discuss what style of combat your party enjoys during Session 0.

Encounter Difficulties

Having varying levels of difficulty in your combat encounters helps the party stay on their toes while still getting to feel strong.

Whether you are preparing an encounter ahead of time or designing one right in the moment, here is some advice to help balance your encounters.

Easy: Easy encounters pose only a small real threat to the party. Enemies should typically be weaker than the party unless there are only a few of them. Characters can generally defeat an enemy in 1 or 2 actions while enemies may struggle to deal critical damage to the party. A small band of goblins makes for a great Easy encounter.

Medium: The most common type of combat encounter, medium difficulty encounters should provide a true challenge to your party and force them to make interesting decisions. Enemies may be stronger than individual party members, especially when dealing with only a few, tough enemies. It should take your characters longer to get through the enemies, and enemies should deal more damage to your characters. A group of bandits lying in wait on the road to ambush the party might be a challenging Medium encounter.

Hard: Difficult encounters testing the limits of your party. Your "Boss fights." These should pose a threat to your party as a whole if not taken seriously. Enemies may be significantly stronger than your characters and capable of dealing tremendous damage. Hard encounters can range from a powerful Archmage to demi-gods and dragons.

Action Economy

Simply put, "action economy" is the number of actions available to each opposing side during combat. Adjusting the action economy of the enemies in combat can dramatically affect the difficulty of the encounter as even a very strong party of characters can quickly find themselves overrun by superior numbers.

For a medium-difficulty encounter, the action economy at the start of the encounter should be roughly balanced between the party and the enemies. From there, it is easy to adjust up or down for easier or more difficult combats.

For example: If you want to run an easy combat with a large number of enemies, then, considering action economy, those enemies may act as a "swarm" and only take 1 action as a group.

On the other hand, if you want to run a "boss" encounter with one, very strong enemy, then giving them additional actions during each round can help even out the action economy and make them more of a threat to your party.

Designing Enemies

The enemies you may face in your journeys are as varied and diverse as the stories you can tell within the NU. A few sample enemies to include in your games are presented later in the next section, but here are some guidelines for creating challenging and memorable enemies of your own.

When designing enemies for your encounters, be sure the enemy you're creating makes sense to be in the story narratively. Encounters with enemies and wandering creatures can be a great way to give your party information about the world they're a part of.

It is also important to consider the motive and any alternatives an enemy may have. What is their reason for sticking around to fight? What would make them give up and run away? Do they have any other options available, like calling for help?

When selecting skills and abilities to give your enemies, select ones you can combine effectively with other enemies in the encounter. Alternatively, you may run enemy combatants without set Skills, similar to how players use Skills in the Quick Start Guide located in **Appendix A.**
(*Note:* To make your enemies feel more unique, consider adding Skills from different class lists to create interesting combos!)

Enemies are broken down into 4 categories in order to assign their Skills and abilities.

Minions: Weak, low level enemies, often dealt with in a single hit. Minions can serve as the main force for an easier encounter, or fight alongside more powerful foes to give them an appearance of authority.

Minions typically have access to 1 or 2 Offensive Skills and 1 Defensive Skill. Their 2 most important abilities are 12, while the rest are 8.

Grunts: Grunts represent the bulk of enemies your party might face. They often possess different sets of Skills and Spells, allowing them to work together effectively in small teams.

Grunts may possess 2-4 Offensive Skills and 1-2 Defensive Skills. Their 2 most important abilities are 14, while the rest are 10.

Elite: Elite enemies pose a greater threat to your party and often lead other groups of enemies into battle. They possess abilities capable of turning the tide of combat if not dealt with quickly.

Give your elite enemies a wide variety of Skills to suit a number of situations, including 1 or 2 signature Skills of an improved level. Elite enemies may also possess multiple Defensive actions, also at higher levels. Their most important ability score is 16. Their second and third most important scores are 14, and the rest are 10.

Boss: Serving as main antagonists in your story, Boss enemies may be an entire combat encounter in their own right.

Boss enemies should have a number of powerful Skills at their disposal, as well as enough Defensive actions to ensure they can pose a proper threat to your party. Bosses are often capable of taking multiple actions each round to keep up with the party.

They most important ability score should be between 18 and 20 depending on the difficulty of the boss. Their second and third most important scores are 16 and 14. The others are 12 except for their weakest score which should be an 8.

Example Combat Round

The following section contains a breakdown of a full round of combat to help you get a sense of how it should flow in your games.

Our party - a Fighter and a Mage - are fighting 2 bandits they've encountered. At the beginning of combat, all 4 combatants roll a d20 to determine Combat Order.

Our Fighter rolls a 19, the highest overall, and wins first action for our party. The Fighter acts first, and makes in to use their *Disarm* Skill against one of the bandits. *Disarm* is decided by a Contested Skill Check, so our Fighter and the Bandit both roll a Skill Check using their Offense Rating. For this example, let's say both their ORs are 10. On the Skill Check, our Fighter rolls

an 8 while the bandit rolls a 3. Because our Figher rolled closer to their actual OR score, they win the Skill Check and the bandit drops their weapon.

Our Mage acts second and casts Cryomancy to attempt to freeze the 2nd bandit to the ground. The Bandit uses their Defensive action to attempt to use the *Dodge* Skill and avoid our Mage's Spell. The bandit is successful in their Dexterity Skill Check, so they avoid the Spell and any Negative effects.

Now it is the Bandit's turn. The first bandit is unarmed and must make a decision. Will they attempt to get their weapon, grapple with the Fighter, or even flee? This is your decision as the Narrator and you should use whatever situational and environmental factors you have to make the call.[19]

For this example, the bandit will draw their secondary weapon - a knife - to continue fighting, however cannot take an Offensive action due to the *Disarm* Skill's effect. The 2nd bandit used their action for this round to defend against our Mage's Spell, so they do not get to act on their turn.

Now it is our party's turn again. The Fighter attacks the bandit and makes a successful Skill Check with their OR. The bandit chooses not to defend, saving their action for the next round, so our Figher makes a Fate Roll to determine damage. They roll high, and deal 60% of the bandit's current HP as damage.

Now it is our Mage's turn again. They decide to use the Summoning Spell to conjure a small flame elemental to turn the numbers in our party's favor. They spend

---

[19] Fate Rolls too!

the mana and make a Fate Roll, however this time it is a low roll providing a poor outcome. They Spell still functions, but they do not summon the ally they were hoping for - instead of the flame elemental, maybe they summon a charcoal elemental instead.

After our party acts, it is the bandits' turn once again. Combat continues this way until all the combatants on one side are incapacitated or until a narratively satisfying outcome is reached.

Sample Combat Encounters

The following section contains sample social encounters you can use in your game, or as a guideline to create your own.

Unofficial Toll

While traveling on the road your party comes to a toll booth that isn't normally there. A bandit approaches their wagon, demanding MP to let them pass safely. Even a quick glance to the treeline near the road shows more bandits lying in wait. They were never planning on letting your party pass safely.

This encounter is great for low level parties still getting used to combat in the NU. It consists mainly of weaker bandits, with 1 bandit captain in the lead. The main advantage the bandits have here is positioning, as they start the encounter surrounding the party. The party can either defend their wagon from all sides, or try to break through the toll booth to escape. Use the stats below for the enemies:

Bandits:
Health Points: 6

Str: 12	Int: 8
Dex: 8	Wis: 8
Con: 8	Cha: 8

OR: 12

Skills:
- Disarm
- Dodge 1/encounter
- Fight Dirty

Bandit Captain:
Health Points: 15

Str: 14	Int: 10
Dex: 10	Wis: 10
Con: 10	Cha: 10

OR: 14

Skills:
- Backstab (25%)
- Cooperative
- Disarm
- Dodge 2/encounter
- Fight Dirty
- Parry (with shield)

Holy Disgrace

The High Priest of a local temple isn't really who they're pretending to be. Corrupted by beings from the lower realms, this Priest has been corrupting their congregation in preparation for an unholy ritual.

The Priest is a dangerous enemy with spellcasting, assisted by 2 demons summoned from the lower realms. This encounter can serve as a boss for lower level parties, or a difficult encounter for more advanced parties.

Use the stats below for the enemies:

Corrupt Priest:
Health Points: 20
Str: 10   Int: 14
Dex: 10   Wis: 16
Con: 10   Cha: 14
OR: 10
Skills:

- Confession
- Defensive Casting
- Righteous Flame
- Slippery Mind
- Unholy Rebuke

Spells:

- Hex
- Summon Planar Ally 1
- Summon Planar Ally 2 - Used to summon demons

Special: The High Priest may take 2 actions per round.

Demons:
Health Points: 35
Str: 14   Int: 10
Dex: 10   Wis: 10
Con: 10   Cha: 10
OR: 14
Skills:

- Dire Charge
- Energy Resistance: Fire
- Parry
- Rending Attack
- Spellcasting Harrier

Spells:

- Pyromancy 2

Fire & Flames

Protecting a vast trove of treasures deep within a mountain[20] slumbers a beast. Intelligent, fierce, and older than any monarch. Only a fool would enter their lair and willingly disturb…the dragon.

Dragons are a staple of the fantasy genre and can prove to be terrifying villains for your games. Below is a sample dragon you can use in the NU, though you should adjust its magic and attacks based on the type of dragon you wish to present in your game.

Dragon:
Health Points: 125
Str: 16   Int: 14
Dex: 8   Wis: 12
Con: 12   Cha: 18
OR: 14
Skills:

- Cause Fear - Superior
- Defensive Casting
- Dire Charge
- Devestating Critical
- Energy Resistance: Fire
- Legendary Armored Skin
- Mage's Disruption
- Rending Attack
- Self-Righteous Flame - Improved (Flame breath attack)
- Spellcasting Harrier
- Parry

Spells:

- Genetic Manipulation 3
- Pyromancy 1, 2, & 3
-
- Time Heal 1/encounter
- Time Stop 1/encounter

Special: Dragons are capable of flight. They gain 2 free offensive and defensive actions each round. Each offensive action or attack may target 1 additional enemy.

Vorpal Bunny

A common threat in the NU, the Vorpal Bunny appears to be an ordinary white rabbit…until it bites you head off.

---

[20] Maybe its misty, I don't know

Vorpal Bunny:
Health Points: 150
Str: 16   Int: 8
Dex: 14   Wis: 8
Con: 12   Cha: 18
OR: 20
Skills:
- Acrobatics
- Armored Skin - Improved
- Devastating Critical
- Dodge
- Improved Critical Strike
- Improved Skill Critical
- Mobility
- Overwhelming Critical
- Parry
- Rending Attack
- Wrestling (with its teeth)

Sloan, Undead Rotbender Druid

Chapter 10: Skills

"Skill" is a very broad term in the Narrative Universe defined as any ability or action your character can use that isn't a Spell. Skills are the primary way your characters will interact with the world and the story.

Using your Skills

Your character's Skills represent abilities and talents practiced, and eventually mastered, over the course of your adventures. What skills you choose and how you use them will have a huge impact on the fate of your character and the story of the party.

Whenever your character takes an action you may use one or more of your Skills. Consult your character's list of trained Skills and tell the Narrator which you would like to attempt, and how your character is utilizing that Skill.

Each Skill in the NU has a variety of ways it can be used both in and out of combat. Under each Skill is listed the action type that Skill is generally most useful for, but it is largely up to the player to find creative ways to apply the Skills they have on hand.

On the rare occasion that a Skill does not apply to a specific task, the Narrator has the discretion to not allow that Skill to be used. However, the NU values and rewards creativity in overcoming narrative obstacles, so this situation should rarely arise except in the case of a major misunderstanding of a given Skill.

Throughout the game, the Narrator may reward Bonuses or impose Penalties on Skill Checks depending on the situation, just as they would Fate Rolls. These normally modify your character's effective ability score when determining the outcome of a Skill Check.

For Example: If your character is attempting to use the *Focus* Skill in a crowded bar, the Narrator might impose a Penalty to the Skill Check, temporarily reducing your Wisdom score by 2 for this Skill Check.

Rolling Skill Checks:

Whenever the Narrator tells you to make a Skill Check, first consult your Skill's reliant abilities. The reliant abilities tell you which ability scores you will use to determine if your Skill Check is successful.

Next, roll a 20-sided die for each of that Skill's reliant abilities. The NU utilizes a roll-under dice mechanic. This means that a success for a Skill Check is any roll *equal to or lower than* your character's ability score.

For example: Let's say you wanted to use the Bard skill *Allegro*, which has a reliant ability of Wisdom. For this example, let's say your character's Wisdom ability score is 12. You would roll one d20 for your Skill Check, and if you roll a 12 or lower, you succeed in the Skill Check. If you roll a 13 or higher on the d20, the Skill Check fails. On a roll directly equal to your ability score (12 in this Example), you score a critical success, and the Narrator may grant additional bonuses to the roll, such as increased damage or an extra non-damaging effect for your Skill.

You may attempt to use Skills from your class list you are not trained in, however, when making a Skill Check for an untrained Skill, your ability score is halved for the purposes of determining success and failure.

Contested Skill Checks

Occasionally Skills will pit your abilities directly against those of your opponent. This is called a Contested Skill Check and requires both parties involved make a Skill Check using the abilities listed in the Skill's description.

The goal is to get as close to your ability score as possible without going over. If you roll a result higher than your ability score, you fail the Contested Skill Check. If both parties fail their Skill Check, it is up to the Narrator to determine the outcome. If both parties succeed in their Skill Check, then whoever rolls closer to their actual ability score is considered the winner. In the case of a tie, or if both parties score a critical success, the Skill Check is repeated until there is a victor.

Contested Skill Checks most commonly occur when your characters are attempting to interfere with the abilities of their opponents, but as the Narrator you can use Contested Skill Checks in many situations. An arm wrestling contest, for example, could easily be settled by a Contested Skill Check.

Contested Skill Checks don't always need to have the same ability rolled by both parties. Feel free to adjust the abilities used in a Contested Skill Check as the Narrator. A character trying to detect if an opponent is bluffing, for example, may make a Contested Skill Check using their Wisdom against the opponent's Charisma.

Group Skill Checks

Sometimes it is wiser to combine your efforts as a group towards a single outcome. Group Skill Checks utilize a different Skill from each party member, risking your overall success or failure as a group.

Whenever your party makes a Group Skill Check, each party member chooses 1 Skill they think will best help with the situation. Everyone makes their Skill Checks together, and tells the Narrator their result. To succeed a Group Skill Check, *more than half* of the party members must succeed their individual Skill Checks.

Alternative: As Narrator, you may treat each individual success or failure as a separate Bonus or Penalty. After all party members have made their Skill Checks, combine all Bonuses and Penalties and make a single Fate Roll to determine the outcome.

Learning New Skills

Learning new Skills in the NU is not just tied to leveling up your character. During preparation rounds, your character may attempt to learn new Skills or improve the ones they already have. You may only attempt to learn new Skills present on your character's class Skill list.
First pick the Skill you would like to attempt to train, then roll 5 Skill Checks for each of the Skill's reliant abilities. You must succeed 5 total Skill Checks for each reliant ability to permanently gain or improve a Skill.

If you do not succeed on all 5 Skill Checks on your first attempt, record any successes you did achieve on your character sheet.

When you attempt to train the same Skill again in the future, you may count any previous successes already made.

For Example: The Narrator asks you if you would like to practice any new Skills while your party travels on the road. You choose the Bard skill *Appraise,* which has the Reliant Abilities of Intelligence and Wisdom.

First, you roll 5 Intelligence Skill Checks and 5 Wisdom Skill Checks. For this example, let's say you rolled 5 successful Intelligence Skill Checks, and 2 successful Wisdom Skill checks. Record those successes on your character sheet. Since you have already succeeded on 5 Intelligence and 2 Wisdom Skill Checks, the next time you attempt to learn *Appraise* you only need to succeed on 3 Wisdom Skill Checks to permanently add it to your sheet.

Alternative: If your Narrator wishes, you may count a critical success on a Skill Check to train a new skill as 2 successes instead of 1, and apply the additional success to any Reliant Ability you like. This makes it easier for players to gain skills with reliant abilities their character do not excel at.

Improving Your Skills

Instead of learning a new Skill, you may attempt instead to improve a Skill you already know. Similar to learning a new Skill, you must again roll 5 successful Skill Checks for each of the Skill's reliant abilities, with any successful rolls carrying over between attempts.

There are 5 improved levels for each Skill:
- Improved - available at Level 5
- Superior - available at Level 10

- Epic - available at Level 15
- Legendary - available at Level 20
- Godlike - available at Level 30

These tiers represent your character's broad understanding and mastery of a Skill, and allow you to use it to greater effect.

Certain Skills have effects listed for what your character gains at advanced levels. For others, they generally represent greater feats your character can achieve with the Skill, left to your Narrator's discretion.

For Example: A Druid with the *Druidic Familiar* Skill might be able to call ordinary woodland creatures to be their companions, but once increased to the *Epic* level, they may be able to call upon elementals and magical creatures. A high level Druid with the *Godlike Druidic Familiar* Skill might have a Dragon or very powerful Forest Spirit as their familiar.

As a general guideline:
- Skills with a limited number of uses per encounter may be used an additional time each encounter with every improved level.
- Skills that grant Bonuses or Penalties may grant larger bonuses or penalties.
- Skills representing your character's background may provide increased reputation or higher social status.

Action Types

While Skills can be used under a variety of circumstances, each Skill has an action type listed that defines the type of encounter it will typically be most useful in. Skills can be used outside the encounter or round suggested by their action type, though your

Narrator may limit the usage of certain Skills depending on the situation[21].

The types of actions you will see in the skill list are:

Preparation: These Skills take a long period of uninterrupted focus to use to their full effect, and are generally used to prepare for the adventuring day ahead.

Exploration: Many exploration Skills are focused on utility and gathering information about your current environment, as well as helping your party navigate dungeons and dangerous terrain.

Social: These Skills are designed to help your characters navigate social encounters and help improve the Attitude of NPCs you meet.

Enduring Feature: These Skills grant a passive bonus and do not require a Skill Check.

Utility These Skills can be used during any round or encounter, often in conjunction with other Skills to increase their effectiveness.

Free: These are special bonus actions that are granted circumstantially by other Skills or abilities (such as the Fighter's Core Ability)

Offensive: Offensive Skills are combat skills meant to deal damage or incapacitate your enemy.

Defensive: Combat skills allowing you to avoid attacks or aid your allies.

____

[21] Dangling from the side of a cliff isn't the best time to dig into some research

(Note: During combat, most classes can use either 1 offensive or 1 defensive action each round. Fighters, however, get 1 free defensive action each round.)

Reading the Skill List

The following chapter contains a complete list of Skills already created by other players in the NU. They are formatted in the following way:

Skill's Name
Requirements: Typically the minimum level your character must be to train the Skill
Classes: The classes that have access to this Skill
Action: The type of encounter or round this Skill will typically be used during
Reliant Abilities: The ability scores used during Skill Checks pertaining to this Skill

[Description of the Skill: Remember, these are just guidelines for Skill usage, and players are able to use their Skills in unique and creative ways.]

Some skills may have "Special" listed as its action or reliant ability. These Skills have specific rules defined within Skill description.

Creating New Skills

The Skill list in the following chapter represents a list of options readily available for your characters and games. If you find a Skill you would like to use for your character that does not already exist in the game, talk with your Narrator and work to create a new Skill.

Creating new Skills for the NU is easy if you use the Skill template above and follow the steps below:

- Pick a name for your new Skill.
- Describe the effect of the new Skill in the game. Most Skills require a Skill check to be used unless they are an Enduring Feature.
- Determine what classes it makes sense to have access to this new Skill.
- Decide what sort of action best suits the Skill. Refer to the **Action Types** section earlier in this chapter.
- Choose reliant abilities the Skill will most consistently use for Skill Checks. Most Skills have 1 or 2 reliant abilities.
- Finally, determine if there are any requirements appropriate for your new Skill. More powerful Skills may have a level requirement attached to them, or require the character make certain role-playing choices in game.

Similar to but legally distinct from *Ricky Span

Chapter 11: Skill List

Note: All skills presented in this chapter were created over time by players of the NU system. You are always free to create and add your own skills to your games!

A full list of skills available for each class is listed in **Appendix E.**

Able Learner
Classes: All
Action: Preparation
Reliant Abilities: All

Once per day during a preparation round, you may attempt to learn or improve two Skills instead of just one.

When you gain improved levels of Able Learner, you may train one additional skill per preparation round.

Abundant Revelations
Classes: Priest
Action: Preparation
Reliant Abilities: Wisdom

Your connection with your deity grants you visions into the past, the present, and even potential futures.

On a successful Skill Check, you may make a request for information from your deity. The Narrator then makes a Fate Roll in secret and narrates a vision based on its outcome.

Acrobatics
Classes: Bard, Fighter, Rogue
Action: Utility
Reliant Abilities: Dexterity

Acrobatics allows you to utilize unique movement options by using your agility and balance. Once per encounter, you may attempt a Skill Check. On a success, choose one of the following effects, or suggest a new one to your Narrator:
- Gain a free Reposition action on your turn
- Climb, jump, or swing to an area outside your normal reach.
- Use your Defensive action to avoid an attack.
- Gain a free Offensive action this round with a Bonus towards any Fate Roll you make from it.

Alchemy
Classes: Mage
Action: Preparation
Reliant Abilities: Intelligence, Wisdom

While alchemy may seem like magic to the uneducated observer, you know it is more scientific practice than mystic art.

You may use your preparation round to craft potions, transmute metals, and more. Tell the Narrator what you would like to attempt to craft, and make any Skill Checks required. On a success, you may spend any amount of GP you have to create 1 new item.

For more information about crafting new items, see **Chapter 5.**

Allegro

Classes: Bard
Action: Offensive
Reliant Abilities: Charisma

Once per encounter, you may play a fast paced tune to inspire your allies to great haste. On a successful Skill Check, for as long as you are playing the song, all allies who can hear you may take an additional action on each of their turns.

You may use your action during your next round to continue playing *Allegro* without making an additional Skill Check. You may not perform any Skills with the Offensive or Defensive action type while performing *Allegro*, but may still cast Spells through the music you're playing.

Alms for the Poor

Classes: Charlatan
Action: Preparation
Reliant Abilities: Charisma

Whenever you are in a town or city, you may spend a preparation round asking for donations from passersby. On a successful Skill Check, roll a d100 and gain twice that amount of MP. On a failure, roll a d20 and gain an equal amount of MP instead.

Ambush

Classes: Fighter, Rogue
Action: Special
Reliant Abilities: Dexterity, Wisdom

If you are able to spend at least 10 minutes ahead of a combat encounter without your enemy becoming aware of your presence, you may attempt to set an ambush.

Make a Skill Check, on a success, your side automatically acts first in combat, and receives a Bonus to any Fate Rolls they make during their first turn.

Animal Languages

Classes: Druid
Action: Exploration
Reliant Abilities: Charisma, Intelligence

You have learned the secret druidic languages, allowing you to communicate with animals in basic ways. On a successful Skill Check, you can communicate with most ordinary animals. You cannot convey any direct messages back and forth, but are able to understand each other's intentions and meaning.

Appraise

Classes: Bard, Mage
Action: Exploration
Dependent Stats: Intelligence, Wisdom

You're skilled at judging an item's value just at a glance. On a successful Skill Check you know a rough estimate of an item's MP value and history.

Archeology

Classes: Bard, Mage, Rogue
Action: Exploration
Reliant Abilities: Intelligence

On a successful Skill Check, Archeology allows you to recall a piece of helpful information regarding the knowledge of maps, ancient temples, lost treasures, or the history of the world.

Armored Skin

Requirement: Level 5
Classes: Fighter
Action: Enduring Feature
Reliant Abilities: Constitution

With a toughness only forged through battle, you are able to shrug off attacks and glancing blows that might wound others.

When you gain this skill, you gain the benefits of light armor without having to wear any. You may only use the armor's ability once per combat, and may not "break" your armored skin.

When you improve armored skin to the Superior level, you gain the benefits of wearing medium armor instead of light. At Legendary, these benefits improve to heavy armor.

Armored Fighting

Classes: Fighter
Action: Enduring Feature
Reliant Abilities: Constitution

You wear your armor like a second skin. You ignore non-magical negative effects from wearing medium and heavy armor, You still may not cast any spells while wearing armor.

Attract Attention

Classes: Charlatan
Action: Social, Defensive
Reliant Abilities: Charisma

On a successful Skill Check, you temporarily become the center of attention for all creatures who are able to see and hear you.
You may choose one of the following effects, or suggest a new one to your Narrator:

- Cause a distraction, giving a Bonus to an ally attempting to go undetected.
- Compel enemy combatants to target you for their next attack.
- Gain the focus of a crowded, noisy room of people.

Aura of Belief

Classes: Charlatan
Action: Utility
Reliant Abilities: Charisma

On a successful Skill Check, you can siphon the faith of a target and wrap yourself in its aura. Until you lose focus on your aura, you are treated as a true believer of the faith of your target. You may only have one aura active at a time.

Aura of belief may be used outside of combat, but may not be used more than once during a single encounter.

Aura of Conviction

Classes: Priest
Action: Offensive
Reliant Abilities: Wisdom

You call upon your deity to steel the nerves of you and your companions. Once per encounter on a successful Skill Check, you may activate your aura. Allies that can see and hear you gain a Bonus against any effect causing them to act against their own will. You may have only one aura active at a time.

Aura of the Divine

Classes: Priest
Action: Defensive
Reliant Abilities: Wisdom

Once per encounter you can call upon your deity to shroud yourself in a protective aura. On a successful Skill Check you are defended from an incoming attack, and enemies opposed to the tenants of your deity are frightened while within your aura. You may only have one aura active at a time.

Aura of Nature

Classes: Druid
Action: Preparation, Defensive
Reliant Abilities: Wisdom

You attune yourself with the spirits of nature surrounding you, warding yourself from unnatural attacks. Until you lose focus on your aura, you damage dealt to you by undead or unnatural enemies if halved.

Aura of Temptation

Classes: Charlatan
Action: Social
Reliant Abilities: Charisma

Your mere presence alone is enough to make even the most devout question their conviction.

Once per encounter on a successful Skill Check, you may activate your aura of temptation. You gain a Bonus to sway the Attitude of any enemy within your aura. You may only have one aura active at a time.

Backstab (10%)

Classes: Rogue
Action: Offensive
Reliant Abilities: Special

Once per encounter you may attempt a devastating attack against an enemy. Make a Skill Check at your current backstab percentage. On a success, you instantly incapacitate weaker enemies or severely weaken stronger ones. Make a Fate Roll to determine the full effect against stronger enemies and bosses.

Backstab is improved by 1% for each successful Skill Check you make while training it, up to a maximum of 80%

Bardic Knowledge

Classes: Bard
Action: Exploration
Dependent Stats: Intelligence, Wisdom

You've heard many stories and tales in your travels, some of them even with a grain of truth to them!

Once per encounter on a successful Skill Check, you may make a Fate Roll to recall the story behind an event or place that you have encountered.

Battle Caster

Requirement: Level 5
Classes: Bard, Charlatan, Druid, Mage, Priest
Action: Enduring Feature
Reliant Abilities: All

Magic can easily turn the tide of combat, and you have learned it is a tide more easily turned from the front lines.

When you gain this skill, you may treat all spellcaster levels as Fighter levels for the sake of learning and training skills.

In addition, when you gain a level from now you gain 1d6 Health Points instead of 1d4, and your Offense Rating now improves every other level.

When you gain Improved Battle Caster, you may wear Light armor while still being able to use your spellcasting ability. At Superior you may wear Medium armor, and at Legendary you may wear Heavy Armor and use shields.

Battle Ready

Classes: Fighter, Rogue
Action: Enduring Feature
Reliant Abilities: Wisdom

You find your hand always resting on your weapon, ready for combat at a moment's notice. For the first round of every combat encounter, you gain one additional Defensive action.

Whenever you improve Battle Ready, you gain this bonus for an additional round at the beginning of combat.

Beastial Aspect

Classes: Druid
Action: Utility
Reliant Abilities: Constitution, Wisdom

You take on the aspects of an animal guardian, granting you both the heightened senses and abilities, and the weaknesses of your chosen animal.

Choose an ordinary animal you are familiar with. On a successful Skill Check, you take on minor physical aspects of that animal for the rest of the day.

For example, if you choose a wolf, you may gain increased speed and sense of smell, but take a Penalty to your eyesight. These attributes are ultimately up to you and your Narrator to determine.

Bolstered Resilience

Classes: Druid, Priest
Action: Defensive
Reliant Abilities: Constitution

You call upon divine healing energies to reinvigorate you and keep you in the fight. Once per encounter as a defensive action, you may attempt a Skill Check. On a success, make a Fate Roll and regain a percentage of your total Health Points equal to the result.

Boundless Optimism

Classes: Priest
Action: Enduring Feature
Reliant Abilities: Charisma

Through your eyes, the world and all its people is a wonderful place. Your boundless optimism has drawn the attention of more benevolent divine beings. You gain a Bonus to any Fate Rolls you make during social encounters with these beings.

Braced Strike

Classes: Fighter
Action: Offensive
Reliant Abilities: Offense Rating

You plant your weapon into the ground, bracing it to strike a charging opponent. Once per encounter on your turn you may forgo your action and instead brace your weapon. If an enemy charges you, or moves into your range while mounted, you may make an attack against them. If this attack hits, double the damage you deal with it.

Branded for Retribution

Classes: Priest
Action: Utility
Reliant Abilities: Wisdom

You brand your opponent with a mark of divine energy, ensuring they do not escape your divine justice. Once per encounter when you hit an enemy with a melee attack, you may attempt a Skill Check to brand the enemy.

While an enemy is branded, you always know the direction towards them as well as their relative distance. The brand can only be removed through magical intervention, or if you place your brand on another target. You may only have one brand active at a time.

Breadth of Experience

Classes: Bard, Druid, Priest
Action: Enduring Feature
Reliant Abilities: All

Whenever you attempt a skill you do not have training for, roll your Skill Check as though your ability score was ¾ it's full amount rather than ½.

Break Action Sequence

Classes: Fighter, Rogue
Action: Defensive
Reliant Abilities: Wisdom

Once per encounter, when an enemy attempts an action utilizing more than a single skill, you may limit their action to only the first skill used.

Called Shot

Classes: Fighter
Action: Enduring Feature
Reliant Abilities: Dexterity, Intelligence

With precision you strike at an opponent's vital spot, inflicting a critical wound to your enemy... if you hit.

Whenever you make an attack, you can choose to call your shot for a specific target on your enemy. If you roll within your crit range, the attack succeeds and your enemy is crippled. However, if you roll outside your crit range the attack misses, even if it would otherwise hit.

Your effective crit range for Called Shot is increased by 1 each time you improve this skill.

Cannot be Deleted

Requirements: Level 7
Classes: All
Action: Enduring feature
Reliant Abilities: Constitution, Wisdom

You have become a fixture of the universe. Spells or effects that would erase you from existence do not function on you.

Cannot be Disintegrated

Requirements: Level 10
Classes: All
Action: Enduring feature
Reliant Abilities: Constitution

Your body is able to resist forces that would tear others apart. Effects and spells causing disintegration do not work on you.

Cannot be Unmade

Requirements: Level 15
Classes: All
Action: Enduring Feature
Reliant Abilities: Constitution, Charisma

Your presence in the universe is fixed and cannot be altered except by the mightiest of powers. You are immune to effects that would wipe your existence away from the timeline.

Can't Hit that Face

Classes: Bard, Charlatan, Druid, Priest
Action: Defensive
Reliant Abilities: Charisma

Once per encounter when you are targeted by an attack, you may use your defensive action to attempt a Skill Check. On a success, the enemy takes pity on you and the attack misses.

Cause Fear

Classes: Charlatan
Action: Offensive
Reliant Abilities: Charisma

Once per encounter you can attempt to reach into an enemies mind and bring their deepest fears to the surface. On a successful Skill Check you frighten one target, weakening their mental resolve and giving them a Penalty to all Skill Checks.

Improved levels of cause fear allow you to affect additional targets with this skill.

Certainty

Requirements: Level 5
Classes: All
Action: Enduring feature
Reliant Abilities: Wisdom

Your beliefs, knowledge, and convictions cannot be called into question. You gain a Bonus against any effects causing you to doubt or act against your sincerely held beliefs.

Channel Nature's Power

Classes: Druid
Action: Offensive
Reliant Abilities: Constitution, Wisdom

You channel the destructive powers of nature into a single, devastating blow. Once per encounter you may attempt a Skill Check to attack an opponent. If you succeed, the damage you deal from the attack is doubled.

Charge of the Herd Beast

Classes: Druid
Action: Offensive
Reliant Abilities: Strength

Once per encounter you may summon the power of a stampede of beasts. On a successful Skill Check, your next attack knocks all enemies it hits backwards.

Charismatic Liar

Classes: Bard, Charlatan, Rogue
Action: Social
Reliant Abilities: Charisma

Whenever you make a Skill Check to lie or make a deception, you may attempt an additional Skill Check at half your Charisma score to gain an extra Bonus to your Fate Roll.

Circle Initiate

Classes: Druid
Action: Enduring Feature
Reliant Abilities: Wisdom, Charisma
You have been initiated into a circle of druids, marking yourself as one of their members. The druid circle will provide support and information to you appropriate to your rank within the circle.

Improved levels of Circle Initiate represent higher ranks within your circle's leadership.

Climbing

Classes: All
Action: Exploration
Reliant Abilities: Strength, Constitution

On a successful Skill Check, you are able to use your action to climb a nearby surface or structure provided it has reasonable places to hold yourself. You may not, for instance, climb a sheer vertical surface, but you may climb a rocky hillside.

Combat Expertise

Classes: Fighter
Action: Utility
Reliant Abilities: Intelligence

Your knowledge of battlefield tactics give you an advantage when attempting to read enemy movements. Once per encounter you may attempt a Skill Check. On a success, you learn the enemy's strategy as well as their targets for the next round of combat.

Combat Readiness

Classes: Fighter, Rogue
Action: Enduring Feature
Reliant Abilities: Dexterity

Whenever you roll at the beginning of combat to determine who acts first, add 1 to your result. This bonus is increased by 1 for every improved level of this skill.

Commander

Classes: Fighter
Action: Utility
Reliant Abilities: Charisma

Once per encounter you may share one of your skills with up to five creatures who can see and hear you. For the duration of the encounter, any affected creature can use the selected skill as though they were trained with it at your current level.

Commune with Deity

Classes: Priest, Druid
Action: Preparation
Reliant Abilities: Intelligence, Charisma

Praying is no longer a one-sided form of communication for you. Now when you talk to them, they talk back.

You may spend a preparation round attempting to commune directly with your deity. On a successful Skill Check, you speak with your god, gaining helpful information, guidance, or advice depending on the outcome of a Fate Roll.

Commune with Nature

Classes: Druid
Action: Exploration
Reliant Abilities: Wisdom, Charisma

You attempt to commune with the natural spirits of your surroundings. Though they are often easier to contact, they are also less powerful beings and more limited in scope than a deity.
On a successful Skill Check, you make contact with the nature spirits, gaining a useful piece of information or guidance without the need of a Fate Roll.

Commune with Random Deity

Classes: Charlatan
Action: Preparation
Reliant Abilities: Charisma

You reach out to any divine being willing to listen to your pleas. On a successful Skill Check, a random deity answers, responding appropriately. The Narrator makes a Fate Roll to determine which deity responds to the Charlatan's request for assistance.

Concentration

Classes: Charlatan, Druid, Mage, Priest
Action: Preparation, Defensive
Reliant Abilities: Wisdom

Your heartbeat slows as the world around you seems to disappear, your focus honing in on your current objective.

On a successful Skill Check, you gain a Bonus during a preparation round to any Fate Rolls regarding research or training you undertake.

When used as a defensive action, you gain a Bonus to resist mental attacks or to maintain the effects of a spell.

Confession

Classes: Priest
Action: Defensive
Reliant Abilities: Wisdom
Once per encounter, you may attempt to compel a target to confess their sins against your deity. Make a Contested Skill Check against the target's Wisdom. On a success, the target must stop and confess their sins before taking further action.

Confusing Revelations
Classes: Charlatan
Action: Preparation
Reliant Abilities: Wisdom

You attempt to peer into the visions of other oracles, gleaming a piece of knowledge never intended for you. On a successful Skill Check, you may make a Fate Roll. The Narrator gives you a random vision of future events depending on the outcome. These visions are never as clear as visions received directly from a deity, and often shrouded in mystery.

Contingency Plan
Requirements: Level 7
Classes: Mage
Action: Preparation
Reliant Abilities: Intelligence, Wisdom

You infuse magical essence into mundane items, storing spells you can drop at a moment's notice.

You may spend a preparation round attempting to craft a contingency plan. You must spend enough mana to cast the spell, as well as gathering points in order to infuse the item with magic. Follow all other rules for crafting items during a preparation round.

When you successfully craft a contingency plan, you may choose a specific trigger, such as reaching 0 hp or being targeted by an attack. When the contingency's trigger occurs, the spell is cast automatically as a free action. Alternatively, you may choose to activate the contingency plan as an action on your turn. Once the spell has been cast, the contingency is spent and any items involved in the casting become ordinary again.

Conviction
Requirements: Level 15
Classes: Priest
Action: Enduring Feature
Reliant Abilities: Wisdom

You embody your deity's tenants with your whole being, your faith cannot be called into question.

Once per encounter, you may automatically succeed a Skill Check made against another divine spellcaster.

Cooperative
Classes: All
Action: Utility
Reliant Abilities: Wis

You can seamlessly combine your skills with those of your allies, allowing you to combine them to greater effect.
This skill may be taken multiple times, each time allowing you to cooperate with a different class. Whenever you attempt a Skill Check with an ally of a chosen class, you gain a Bonus to any Fate Roll made as a result of your action.

Countersong
Classes: Bard
Action: Defensive
Reliant Abilities: Intelligence, Charisma

You play a discordant melody, briefly interrupting a spellcaster's connection to the other realms. Once per encounter as a defensive action, you may force an enemy spellcaster to make a Contested Skill Check against your Charisma to successfully cast their spell. If they fail, any costs to cast the spell are still spent but it has no effect. Mages use Intelligence for the Contested Skill Check, other Bards and Charlatans use Charisma, and Priests and Druids use their Wisdom.

Crack in the Defenses

Classes: Fighter, Rogue
Action: Utility
Reliant Abilities: Int

Your experience on the battlefield allows you to detect an enemy's potential weakness in an instant. Once per encounter you may attempt a Skill Check to deduce a target's weaknesses. On a success, you learn any weaknesses or vulnerabilities the target has.

Crafting

Classes: All
Action: Preparation
Reliant Abilities: Special

When you gain this skill, choose one craft or trade to specialize in. You gain the ability to craft non-magical items of your craft or trade using gathering points during a preparation round.

Each time you take this skill, you may choose a different craft or trade to specialize in. Improved levels of this skill allow you to craft items of higher equipment value.

The reliant abilities of this skill are dependent on the selected craft or trade, and chosen by the Narrator. Follow the advice in the **Crafting** section of **Chapter 5** on setting these abilities.

Create Opportunity

Classes: All
Action: Defensive, Utility
Reliant Abilities: Wisdom

Once per encounter, you may attempt to create an opportunity, granting an ally an extra action they may take immediately.

Alternatively, you may use *Create Opportunity* as a Defensive action whenever an ally fails their Skill Check. If you make a successful Skill Check, you give up your next turn's action and the ally may reroll their failed Skill Check.

Cult Leader

Requirements: Level 10
Classes: Charlatan, Priest
Action: Enduring Feature
Reliant Abilities: Charisma

You draw people to your cause, amassing a small following that consider you their leader and sage. You may attempt to gain new followers wherever you travel by spending a preparation round preaching. Make a Skill Check and on a success, you convert at least 1 new member to your following.

Your followers will attempt to aid you in your travels, providing MP and GP when they are able. During a preparation round you may make a Fate Roll and gain either MP or GP equal to the result. Your most devout followers may even wade into battle and give their lives at your side.

Damage Reduction

Requirement: Level 10
Classes: Fighter
Action: Enduring Feature
Reliant Abilities: Constitution

Your resolve in combat is unwavering, allowing you to shrug off wounds and keep yourself upright. Whenever you take damage you may roll a d100 and reduce the incoming damage by an equal percentage.

Death Bless

Requirements: Level 5
Classes: Charlatan, Druid, Priest
Action: Enduring Feature
Reliant Abilities: All

Upon your death, you channel the last of your remaining lifeforce into a radiant burst of energy, reinvigorating your allies.

You may choose to forego any chance of resurrection upon your death. In exchange, all nearby allies are healed to full health and regain any spent abilities and mana as if it were the start of a new day. They also gain a Bonus to any Fate Rolls made for the rest of the encounter.

After this ability has been activated, your body and belongings are reduced to a small pile of ash and your soul is permanently tied to the realm of the dead.

Death Curse

Requirements: Level 5
Classes: Charlatan, Druid, Priest
Action: Enduring Feature
Reliant Abilities: All

You unleash a terrible curse upon your enemies at the time of your death, pouring any remaining life energy into a devastating, often deadly attack.

You may choose to forego any chance of resurrection upon your death. In exchange, all enemies in the area suffer the effects of a terrible curse. You may make a suggestion for the curse's effects upon your death, and then make a Fate Roll. The curse's effects are proportionate to the result of the Fate Roll.

After this ability has been activated, your body and belongings are reduced to a small pile of ash and your soul is permanently tied to the realm of the dead.

Deathless

Requirements: Level 10
Classes: All
Action: Enduring Feature
Reliant Abilities: All

You have danced with death many times and know how to escape her grasp. Once per day whenever you are reduced to 0 hp, you are instead restored to full life.

Deception

Classes: All
Action: Utility
Reliant Abilities: Charisma

On a successful Skill Check, you can effectively lie or hide the truth from most NPCs. If a creature is trying to decipher the truth from your words, they must succeed a Contested Skill Check against your Charisma using their Wisdom.

Decipher Script

Classes: Bard, Mage, Priest, Rogue
Action: Preparation
Reliant Abilities: Intelligence

During a preparation round, you may attempt to study a piece of written language you do not currently understand. On a successful Skill Check, you are able to figure out what the script says. You maintain the ability to read any scripts you have already deciphered, however you are not able to learn the entire language.

Defile

Classes: Druid
Action: Offensive
Reliant Abilities: Wisdom

Once per encounter you may defile a small area around you, draining life from everything nearby and rejuvenating yourself in the process.
On a successful Skill Check, all natural things around you have their life drained, and nearby plants wither and die. You also regain the use of a spent 1st level Prayer.

Defensive Casting

Classes: Bard, Charlatan, Druid, Priest, Mage
Action: Defensive
Reliant Abilities: Intelligence, Wisdom

With quick reflexes you are able to cast a spell to defend yourself. Once per encounter you may quickly cast a spell as a defensive action.

Deflection

Classes: Fighter
Action: Defensive
Reliant Abilities: Dexterity

Once per encounter, when you would be hit by a ranged attack you may attempt a Contested Skill Check against your attacker's Offense Rating. If you are successful, you reduce the damage of the attack to 0.

Demon Hunter

Requirements: Level 5
Classes: Priest
Action: Enduring Feature
Reliant Abilities: Wisdom, Charisma

You have gained a reputation as a demon hunter within your church. Other clergy may seek your guidance or occasionally ask for your help with a mission. In addition, your expertise grants you a Bonus on all rolls relating to hunting demons.

Desperate Prayer
Requirements: Level 15
Classes: Charlatan
Action: Enduring Feature
Reliant Abilities: Charisma

In your hour of need, you call out for help to any deity willing to answer your prayer. And when help comes, it comes with a price. Once per encounter you may cast a prayer without a chance for failure. Make a Fate Roll to determine which deity answers your request. At the Narrator's discretion, the deity may ask for something in exchange for their assistance.

Detect Trap (10%)
Classes: Rogue
Action: Exploration
Reliant Abilities: Special

Your ability to sense a trap lying in wait borders on the uncanny. On a successful Skill Check at your current percentage, you learn about any traps in the nearby area.

Detect Trap is improved by 1% for each successful Skill Check you make while training it, up to a maximum of 80%.

Detect Treasure (10%)
Classes: Rogue
Action: Exploration
Reliant Abilities: Special

A big payday never slips under your nose. On a successful Skill Check, you learn the whereabouts of any valuable treasure or items in the nearby area.

Detect Treasure is improved by 1% for each successful Skill Check you make while training it, up to a maximum of 80%.

Devastating Critical
Classes: Fighter
Action: Enduring Feature
Reliant Abilities: Strength, Offense Rating

Your strikes land with great fury, sending your enemies reeling. Whenever you score a critical hit, any Bonus you gain to the damage of that attack is doubled.

Devil in your Ear
Classes: Charlatan
Action: Enduring Feature
Reliant Abilities: Wisdom

Your prayers have been answered by a dark force, whispering advice into your ear which you embrace with open arms. You gain a Bonus to any Fate Roll made to cause harm or instill fear. Whenever you improve this Skill, the Bonus you gain increases.

Diplomacy
Classes: Bard, Charlatan, Priest, Rogue
Action: Utility
Reliant Abilities: Charisma

With a cool head and an eye for attrition, you are able to work naturally in almost any diplomatic situation.
On a successful Skill Check, you gain a Bonus to any Fate Roll to determine the outcome of diplomatic negotiations.

Dire Charge

Classes: Fighter
Action: Offensive
Reliant Abilities: Strength

Throwing caution to the wind, you rush towards the enemy with a whirlwind attack. You may spend one turn in combat charging directly towards an enemy. If you do so, you gain a Bonus to damage on any attack made against the targeted enemy during your next round.

Disarm

Classes: Fighter
Action: Offensive
Reliant Abilities: Offense Rating

"In a duel, an empty hand is often the losing one..."
Once per encounter, you may attempt to disarm an opponent with a Contested Skill Check against the target's Strength or Dexterity (target's choice). If you succeed the target immediately drops their weapon and cannot take an Offensive action during their next turn.

Disciple of Pain

Classes: Charlatan, Priest
Action: Enduring Feature
Reliant Abilities: Wisdom

Your deity demands blood be shed in their name, and they do not care whose. You gain a Bonus towards any physical damage you deal, as well as Fate Rolls to cause fear.

Distant Shot

Classes: Fighter
Action: Enduring Feature
Reliant Abilities: Dexterity

You are able to quickly adjust your aim to account for the variables of a long distance shot. Whenever you attempt a ranged attack, you may first make a Dexterity Skill Check. On a success, you may target enemies further away than you may normally hit.

Divine Bard

Requirements: Level 10
Classes: Priest
Action: Enduring Feature
Reliant Abilities: Charisma

Your god speaks through you on this realm, turning your passionate sermons into powerful spells.

Once gained, divine bard allows you to cast spells using songs like the bard class. Charisma is the reliant ability of any spells cast this way. You still maintain access to your normal priest spell list and Prayers.

When you gain this skill you immediately gain 5 mana. Every time you gain a level your maximum mana increases by 5. You may use this mana only to cast Variable cost Spells as per the Bard's Musical Spellcasting ability.

Divine Interdiction

Classes: Charlatan, Druid, Priest
Action: Defensive
Reliant Abilities: Wisdom

Through force of will you are able to interrupt another divine spellcaster's spell. Once per encounter as a defensive action, you may attempt a Contested Skill Check against the target's wisdom. If you succeed, the target is unable to cast any divine spells or use any divine skills until their next turn.

Dodge

Classes: Fighter, Rogue
Action: Defensive
Reliant Abilities: Dexterity
Once per encounter you may attempt a Skill Check to move out of the way of an attack or Spell at the last moment. On a success, the damage you are dealt from the attack is reeduced to 0 and you avoid any negative Spell effects.

Druidic Companion

Requirements: Level 2
Classes: Druid
Action: Preparation
Reliant Abilities: Wisdom, Charisma

Animals can sense your strong ties with nature, leading wild creatures to form strong bonds with you. During a preparation round you may attempt a Skill Check to turn an animal into your druidic companion.

Your druidic companion acts as though completely domesticated and loyal towards you. They will obey any of your commands to the best of their abilities, though do not gain any enhanced intelligence or attributes.

Whenever you improve druidic companion you may gain an additional companion.

Druidic Familiar

Requirements: Level 5
Classes: Druid
Action: Preparation
Reliant Abilities: Wisdom

You imbue one of your druidic companions with a portion of your divine abilities. You and your familiar are able to communicate telepathically and understand each other, as well as see through each other's eyes.

During a preparation round, you may store a spell in your familiar by expending your use of it. The spell is stored until it is used or until they are no longer your familiar.

Druidic Rituals

Requirements: Level 7
Classes: Druid
Action: Preparation
Reliant Abilities: All

While mages were still struggling to learn the flow of mana, druids had been practicing magic through rituals for generations. During a preparation round, you may cast a spell as a ritual using gathering points instead of expending its use.

Dual Wielding

Classes: Fighter
Action: Enduring Feature
Reliant Abilities: Strength, Dexterity

"Two's better than one."
You may take an additional offensive or defensive action each round with your

off-hand weapon. This bonus stacks with your free defensive action as a fighter.

Dungeoneering
Classes: Bard, Rogue
Action: Exploration
Reliant Abilities: Intelligence, Wisdom

You are able to navigate your way through even the most labyrinthian dungeons.
You may attempt a Skill Check while within a dungeon or dungeon-like area. On a success you may:
- Note your current path and route to avoid getting lost
- Inspect for structural or environmental dangers
- Try to deduce the history or inhabitants of this place
- Suggest a different option to your Narrator

Efficacious Healer
Classes: Druid, Priest
Action: Enduring Feature
Reliant Abilities: Wisdom

You are a font of healing magic for your allies, ensuring no harm comes to them under your watch. You gain a Bonus to any Fate Roll you make while attempting to heal an individual.

Elementalist
Requirements: Level 4
Classes: Mage
Action: Enduring Feature
Reliant Abilities: Intelligence, Wisdom

You have gained mastery over a particular element, allowing you to infuse it into your spells with ease.

When you gain this skill, choose an element. Whenever you cast a spell, you may infuse the spell with the element you have chosen, altering its effects.

You may take this skill multiple times, choosing a new element each time you do so.

Eminence
Classes: Druid
Action: Preparation
Reliant Abilities: Wisdom

You attune yourself with a specific aspect of nature, causing creatures sharing that aspect to react favorably towards you.
On a successful Skill Check, choose Blue (water), Red (fauna), or Green (flora). You become attuned to the selected color until you attune to a different color. Creatures and beings sharing aspects with your attunement have a more favorable Attitude towards you.

Enchanting
Requirements: Level 5
Classes: Mage
Action: Preparation
Reliant Abilities: Int, Wis

With time and concentration you are able to infuse ordinary objects with extraordinary magical abilities.
You may attempt to enchant an ordinary item during a preparation round. On a successful Skill Check, you may spend

gathering points to enchant an object with one of your spells, permanently enhancing the abilities of the object. See **Chapter 5** for more information on crafting.

Energy Resistance

Classes: Fighter
Action: Enduring Feature
Reliant Abilities: Constitution

Only the most skilled warriors can survive against the forces of magic with only steel. Whenever you gain this skill, choose an element. Whenever you take damage from the chosen element, you take half as much. You may take this skill multiple times, choosing a different element each time you do so.

Endurance

Classes: Fighter
Action: Utility
Reliant Abilities: Constitution

You may attempt a Skill Check to gain a Bonus on any Fate Rolls regarding pushing past the normal limits of your stamina.

In addition, if you are dealt a lethal blow you may attempt to make a Skill Check. On a success, make a Fate Roll to see if you are able to persevere through the injury.

Enhanced Perception

Classes: Any
Action: Enduring Feature
Reliant Abilities: Wisdom

Your senses of perception are heightened to an almost supernatural degree. You gain a

Bonus to any Fate Rolls made to pick our details from your environment.

Enhance Personal Narrative

Classes: Bard
Action: Utility
Reliant Abilities: Wisdom, Charisma

"I swear, that's JUST how it happened…"

Your Bardic magic slips through your words, turning stories into reality. Once per encounter on a successful Skill Check, you gain a Bnus to any Fate Roll related only to yourself.

Evasion (10%)

Classes: Rogue
Action: Defensive
Reliant Abilities: Special

You gain a near sixth sense to avoid damage before it lands. Once per encounter as a defensive action, when you are the target of an attack or spell you may attempt a Skill Check at your current evasion percentage. On a success, any damage you take from the attack or spell is reduced to 0.

Evasion is improved by 1% for each successful Skill Check you make while training it, to a maximum of 80%.

Exorcist

Classes: Priest
Action: Enduring Feature
Reliant Abilities: Wisdom

You have gone up against demons and devils and none have stood against the power of your deity.
You gain a Bonus to Fate Rolls relating to banishing an entity from this Realm of existence.

Extra Mana

Classes: Bard, Mage
Action: Enduring Feature
Reliant Abilities: All

When you take this skill you permanently gain 1 mana for each level in a spellcasting class you have. In addition, whenever you level up you gain 1 additional mana.

Fae Connections

Classes: Druid, Mage
Action: Preparation
Reliant Abilities: Charisma

Your magic shares a connection with the fae, allowing you to call on fae creatures for help and guidance, though it may be on their own terms.
You may spend a preparation round attempting to contact the fae for help. On a successful Skill Check, make a Fate Roll. The Narrator shares a piece of information with you dependent on the outcome.

Fae Ecology

Classes: Bard, Druid, Mage, Rogue
Action: Exploration
Reliant Abilities: Intelligence

You have studied a wide array of topics regarding Fairy type creatures. On a successful Skill Check, you may learn a particular piece of information regarding the general behaviors, feeding habits, environment, or physical stats of fairy creatures.

Fae Protocols

Classes: Bard, Druid, Mage, Rogue
Action: Social
Reliant Abilities: Cha

Fae society is intricate and its norms even more so for the uninitiated. It's easy for an outsider to raise the suspicion, and even anger of the Fae by accident. You may attempt a Skill Check while interacting with fae creatures to understand their customs and communicate more effectively, without the risk of accidentally lowering their Attitude.

Faithful Servant

Classes: Priest
Action: Preparation
Reliant Abilities: Wisdom

You have become an agent for your deity on the mortal realm, carrying out their will wherever you go. During a preparation round, you may attempt a Skill Check to be granted a quest from your deity.

Improved levels of this skill grant additional quests, as well as increased rewards from your deity upon completion.

False Reputation

Classes: Bard, Charlatan
Action: Enduring Feature
Reliant Abilities: Charisma

You have painstakingly built up a reputation for yourself that you, decidedly, do not deserve.

When you gain this skill, talk with your Narrator to determine a reputation suitable for your character. Word of your reputation will spread and you may receive requests from individuals relevant to your background. People are inclined to believe your reputation unless they know or learn otherwise.

Fascinate

Classes: Bard
Action: Defensive, Utility
Reliant Abilities: Charisma

You know how to work a crowd and keep attention focused on you. On a successful Skill Check, roll a d10 and improve their Attitude towards you by an amount equal to the result.

Once per encounter as a defensive action you may attempt a Skill Check to fascinate one target and prevent them from making any attacks for 1 round.

Favored Weapon

Requirements: Level 6
Classes: Fighter
Action: Enduring Feature
Reliant Abilities: Wisdom

Some warriors form a special bond with their weapon, wielding it like an extension of their arm.
When you gain this skill, choose a weapon you own. Whenever you take an offensive or defensive action while using this weapon, you gain a Bonus to any Skill Checks you make.
However, if you lose or are separated from your favored weapon, no other feels quite right in your hand and you take a Penalty on any Fate Rolls made while using a weapon other than your favorite.

Feint

Classes: Fighter
Action: Utility
Reliant Abilities: Intelligence, Charisma

You momentarily distract your opponent, catching them off guard and taking the opportunity to land an attack. Once per encounter you may attempt a Skill Check. On a success you may take a free Offensive action this round and gain a Bonus on its Skill Check.

Fight Dirty

Classes: Fighter, Rogue
Action: Offensive
Reliant Abilities: Dexterity, Wisdom

Kicking shins, throwing sand, poking eyes, in your mind anything goes in a fight.
As an offensive action on your turn, you may attempt a Skill Check to fight dirty. On a success, your attack does no damage but the target must spend their action on their next round dealing with your distraction.

Fighting Blind

Requirement: Level 5
Classes: Fighter
Action: Enduring Feature

Reliant Abilities: Wisdom

You are able to calm your mind and stay in tune with your senses in the heart of battle, to the point where you can still fight effectively even without the use of your eyes.

You ignore any penalties to your offensive and defensive action from not being able to use your eyesight.

Financial Backers
Requirements: Special
Classes: All
Action: Enduring Feature
Reliant Abilities: Charisma

You have some friends with deep pockets, but be wary. Their money often comes with some strings attached.
Financial backers may only be taken at the beginning of the game. You gain an additional 2000 MP per starting level. Consult with your Narrator to determine where this money came from and any connections you may have to its source.

Flexible Prayer
Requirements: Level 12
Classes: Charlatan, Priest
Action: Utility
Reliant Abilities: Intelligence, Wisdom

You gain access to the mage's Sculpt Spell skill and may apply its effects to your divine prayers.

Focus
Classes: Mage
Action: Preparation
Reliant Abilities: Wisdom

When dealing with powerful magical energies it's best to keep your concentration on them. This is a lesson every mage learns early on in their magical studies.

You may attempt to make a Skill Check to prepare a spell. On a success, you may cast the spell once during the next day without spending any mana.

Alternatively, you may use this skill to help aid your magical studies. Whenever you are researching a new spell or crafting magical items, you may attempt a Skill Check to gain a Bonus to that roll.

Foraging
Classes: All
Action: Exploration
Reliant Abilities: Intelligence, Wisdom

Whether out in the wilderness or in the heart of civilization, you have a keen eye for finding what you need to get by. On a successful Skill Check, you can spend an exploration round gathering food, basic supplies, or gathering points from your surroundings.

Forging
Classes: All
Action: Preparation
Reliant Abilities: Strength, Intelligence

With fire and hammer you forge weapons and armor from raw metal, supplying your party with whatever equipment they may need.

During a preparation round, as long as you have access to a forge you can attempt a Skill Check to craft non-magical items using gathering points. See **Chapter 5** for more details on crafting.

Gather Animal Congress

Requirements: Level 10
Classes: Druid
Action: Defensive
Reliant Abilities: Wisdom, Charisma

You call forth a tide of animals from the surrounding area that rush to your defense, overwhelming your enemies. Once per encounter you may attempt a Skill Check as a defensive action. On a success, a large group of animals swarm the area and attempt to stop any enemies from harming you.

When used outside of combat, you may give basic commands to the animals you gather who attempt to follow them to the best of their abilities.

Gather Congregation

Classes: Charlatan, Priest
Action: Preparation
Reliant Abilities: Wisdom, Charisma

With fervor and passion you preach your sermon, gathering a small congregation of believers at your side. You may attempt a Skill Check during a preparation round to gather a religious congregation to aid you.

The congregation will willingly offer small donations or information, but may be worked into a religious fervor to follow you more specifically. You may choose to make a Fate Roll to see how well your congregation responds to your requests.

Gather Elements

Classes: Mage
Action: Preparation
Reliant Abilities: Intelligence, Wisdom

You channel raw elemental power into workable spellcrafting materials. When you search for gathering points during a preparation round, you may attempt a Skill Check to gain a Bonus to your Fate Roll.

Gather Information

Classes: All
Action: Exploration
Reliant Abilities: Intelligence, Charisma

Whether it's keeping an ear open for town gossip, or knowing just the right person to talk to, you are able to gather information about the local area. On a successful Skill Check, make a Fate Roll. The Narrator shares any useful information you collect depending on the result of the roll.

Guided Hand

Classes: Priest
Action: Utility
Reliant Abilities: Wisdom

With blind faith you turn yourself over to your deity, allowing their influence to guide your actions. Once per encounter you may attempt a Skill Check. On a success, the Narrator describes the next action your character does instead of you. Any Fate Rolls made as a result of this action gain a Bonus.

Haggling
Classes: Bard, Rogue
Action: Social
Reliant Abilities: Charisma

With the right influence and a few kind words, no price is ever really final for you. Whenever you are buying equipment or supplies, you may attempt a Skill Check to gain a lower price. On a success, the price is lowered by up to 25% depending on the shopkeeper's Attitude towards you.

Harmful Roast
Classes: Bard, Charlatan
Action: Offensive
Reliant Abilities: Charisma

You wrap your magic around a viscous string of insults you hurl at your enemy, causing them psychic harm. Once per encounter as an offensive action, you may attempt a Skill Check to deal damage to an enemy with your insults.

Hearty
Classes: Fighter
Action: Enduring Feature
Reliant Abilities: Constitution

"Why didn't you tell me they're built like an ox?!"

Whenever your max HP increases, it increases by the maximum amount possible.

Heavy Weapon Fighting
Classes: Fighter
Action: Enduring Feature
Reliant Abilities: Strength

You forgo a shield and grip your massive weapon with both hands, turning yourself into a juggernaut on the battlefield. While you are wielding a weapon with both hands you gain a Bonus to any damage rolls you make with attacks using that weapon.

Hey, I Like Their Vibe
Classes: Bard, Charlatan, Priest, Rogue
Action: Social
Reliant Abilities: Charisma

They say first impressions last a lifetime, and you've learned how to take full advantage of this to make sure you always get off on the right foot.

Whenever you meet a new individual, you may attempt a Skill Check to influence their opinion of you. On a success, their starting Attitude towards you is improved by 1 full increment. However, if you fail this Skill Check, the target's starting Attitude towards you will decrease by a full increment instead.

Hidden Faith

Classes: Charlatan, Druid, Priest
Action: Preparation
Reliant Abilities: Wisdom

Not everywhere is friendly to those of devout faith. You may attempt a Skill Check at the beginning of a preparation round to hide any outward signs of your faith to observers for the entire day.

Historical Knowledge

Classes: Bard, Charlatan, Mage, Priest, Rogue
Action: Exploration
Reliant Abilities: Intelligence

"Those who do not learn from history are doomed." - Ancient Onarian Proverb

You may attempt a Skill Check during an exploration round to recall a piece of historical information related to your surroundings.

Holy Oath

Requirements: Special
Classes: Druid, Priest
Action: Enduring Feature
Reliant Abilities: Special

You pledge yourself totally and completely to your deity, gaining a bonus to all your abilities so long as you follow their tenants. To gain holy oath as a skill you must talk with your Narrator and develop a set of rules and guidelines your character must follow in honor of their deity.

As long as you are following the tenants of your oath, you gain a +1 to all of your ability scores. You lose this bonus if you act in any way contradictory to your oath. To regain the bonus, you must make a penance with your deity as determined by the Narrator.

Holy Rebuke

Classes: Priest
Action: Offensive
Reliant Abilities: Wisdom

You hold the symbol of your deity high in the air, shedding a radiant light that keeps all undead entities at bay. Once per encounter as an offensive action, you may attempt a Skill Check to rebuke any undead or evil creatures in the area. On a success, lesser undead are completely destroyed while stronger undead and evil creatures flee or are held at bay.

Identify Device

Classes: Bard, Mage, Rogue
Action: Exploration
Reliant Abilities: Intelligence

Many devices are dangerous if you don't know how to use them properly. You may attempt a Skill Check to learn about an ordinary device's use and operation.

At improved levels, Identify Device may be used to identify the properties of magical items.

Improved Ability

Requirements: Level 5
Classes: All
Action: Enduring Feature
Reliant Abilities: Special

When you gain this skill, choose 1 ability to use as its reliant ability. Your ability score for the chosen ability increases by 1, up to a maximum of 20.

Improved levels of this skill have an increased level requirement of 5, and improve the chosen ability score by 1 additional point for each level. You may not increase your ability score above 20 this way.

You may take Improved Ability multiple times, choosing a different ability each time you do so.

Improved Critical Strike

Requirements: Level 5
Classes: Fighter
Action: Enduring Feature
Reliant Abilities: Offense Rating

Whenever you roll for an attack, you score a critical hit when you roll your Offense Rating or 1 lower. Each improved level of this skill increases your effective critical strike range by 1.

Improved Skill Critical

Requirement: Level 5
Classes: Any
Action: Enduring Feature
Reliant Abilities: Special

Before you gain improved skill critical, choose one of your ability scores to treat as its reliant ability.

Once gained, whenever you make a Skill Check using the chosen ability, you score a critical success when you roll your ability score or 1 under. Each improved level of this skill increases your critical success range by 1.

Improved Skill Critical may be taken multiple times, choosing a different ability score each time.

Improved Summoning

Classes: Mage
Action: Enduring Feature
Reliant Abilities: Charisma

Your summoned allies are more loyal to you and less likely to rebel against your commands. You gain a Bonus to any Fate Roll you make to determine the actions of one of your summoned creatures.

In the Shadow of your Wings

Requirements: Level 10
Classes: Priest
Action: Defensive
Reliant Abilities: Wisdom

You wrap yourself in shadowy wings, disappearing from the battlefield.

Once per encounter you may attempt a Skill Check to instantly avoid an incoming attack. On a success, you teleport to another space on the battlefield and become Unnoticeable (as per the skill).

Incredible Luck (5%)

Classes: Rogue
Action: Utility
Reliant Abilities: Special

"Fortune favors the lucky."
Once per encounter, you may attempt a Skill Check at your current incredible luck percentage to reroll a Fate Roll made by you or an ally.

Incredible Luck is improved by 1% for each successful Skill Check you make while training it, up to a maximum of 35%.

Innocent Appearance
Classes: Bard, Charlatan, Rogue
Action: Social
Reliant Abilities: Charisma

They say don't judge a book by its cover. Fortunately for you, this is advice many people don't take. You gain a Bonus whenever you make a Skill Check to avoid suspicion against you.

Insight
Classes: All
Action: Social
Reliant Abilities: Wisdom

You can learn a lot about an individual by paying attention to what goes unsaid during a conversation.
You may attempt a Contested Skill Check against a target's Charisma to learn more about their motives and intentions.

Inspire Courage
Classes: Bard
Action: Defensive
Reliant Abilities: Wisdom, Charisma

You play a triumphant melody, bolstering your allies' courage against fear based effects. Once per encounter on a successful Skill Check, you may grant all allies who can hear you a Bonus to their Constitution and Wisdom based Skill Checks.

Intimidation
Classes: All
Action: Social
Reliant Abilities: Charisma

You strike fear into your enemies, causing them to doubt their next actions. Once per encounter you may attempt a Skill Check to cause an enemy to hesitate or fear you.

Investigation
Classes: All
Action: Exploration
Reliant Abilities: Intelligence

You have a keen eye for details, spotting clues others might easily miss. You may attempt a Skill Check to search for clues or hidden details within an object or your surroundings.

Iron Will
Classes: All
Action: Enduring Feature
Reliant Abilities: Wisdom

While some may call you stubborn, you are hard to sway from your way, even through magical effects. You may force an opponent to make a Contested Skill Check using their Wisdom to force you to act against your will through any means, or to have your thoughts read magically.

Jack of All Trades (10%)

Classes: Bard, Rogue
Action: Utility
Reliant Abilities: Special

You have an approximate knowledge of many things. Once per encounter you may attempt a Skill Check at your current jack of all trades percentage. On a success, you can perform any non-magical actions of a skill you are not trained in.

Jack of all trades is improved by 1% for each successful Skill Check you make while training it, up to a maximum of 80%.

Keen Ear

Classes: Bard
Action: Utility
Reliant Abilities: Intelligence

Bards have a well tuned ear, able to pick out details even in a crowded room. On a successful Skill Check, you become more sensitive to sound for a brief time, giving you a Bonus to hear things through a wall or pick out details of a conversation in a crowd.

Lay on Hands

Classes: Charlatan, Druid, Priest
Action: Defensive
Reliant Abilities: Wisdom

Once per encounter you may attempt a Skill Check to call upon your deity to aid an injured party member. Make a Fate Roll to determine the outcome.

Leadership

Classes: Fighter
Action: Utility
Reliant Abilities: Wisdom

You know the strengths and weaknesses of your party members, and more importantly how to lead them in battle. Once per encounter you may attempt a Skill Check to give one of your allies access to a defensive skill you possess.

Legendary Defenses

Requirements: Level 20
Classes: All
Action: Utility
Reliant Abilities: All
You didn't make it this far without learning a trick or two. Three times per encounter, you may automatically succeed any Skill Checks you make related to a single defensive action.

Legerdemain

Classes: Bard
Action: Utility
Reliant Abilities: Dexterity

"Now watch my hands, very closely."

Your skills at performing card tricks to wow the crowd come in *handy*[22] in a number of different ways. On a successful Skill Check you may gain a Bonus on your next attempt to pick-pocket, wriggle loose of bonds, or entertain a crowd with card tricks.

---

[22] I warned you at the beginning of this book there would be more of these

Lesser Demesne
Requirements: Level 15
Classes: Priest
Action: Special, Preparation
Reliant Abilities: Wisdom

You perform a set of sacred rites, forever imbuing your deity's essence into a small piece of land.

Once per level gained at 15 and above, you may spend a preparation round to bless a small area of land, permanently claiming it for your deity. The land slowly begins to change, taking on minor aspects appropriate for your deity. Followers will slowly be drawn to the area as a place of worship.

In addition to granting the benefits of the Hallowed Ground skill to all believers in the area, it is also easier to commune with your deity here, granting you a Bonus on any Fate Rolls made in an attempt to communicate with your deity.

Each time you gain a level you may either choose to bless a new area of land, or to add to an existing Demesne, provided there is enough free space to do so.

Lightning Reflexes
Requirements: Dodge skill
Classes: Fighter, Rogue
Action: Utility
Reliant Abilities: Dexterity

You stay light on your feet in battle, reacting to your enemies nearly instinctively. Once per encounter, you may attempt a Skill Check to gain a Bonus on any Dexterity reliant defensive Skill. You also gain an additional use of the dodge skill each encounter.

Local Connections
Classes: Bard, Rogue
Action: Preparation
Reliant Abilities: Charisma

No matter where you travel, you have a knack for meeting just the right people. You may attempt a Skill Check during a preparation round to gain a Bonus to either searching for gathering points, or finding information.

Local Knowledge
Classes: Bard, Rogue
Action: Exploration
Reliant Abilities: Intelligence

"I'm at least sixty percent sure I've been here before…"

While you are in a city or town, you may attempt a Fate Roll to see how well you know the surrounding area.

Lower Realm Connections
Requirements: Level 6
Classes: Charlatan, Mage, Priest
Action: Preparation
Reliant Abilities: Charisma

Most mages refuse to contact the lower realms out of fear, but you see only opportunity. You are familiar with a demon or a devil of the lower realms and have made a bargain for assistance. The details of this bargain should be agreed upon by you and your Narrator.

During a preparation round you may attempt to summon your contact. On a successful

Skill Check, they answer, and may grant assistance to you at a cost.

Lower Realm Protocols

Classes: Charlatan, Mage, Priest
Action: Social
Reliant Abilities: Charisma

When it comes to dealing with literal devils, it helps to understand how they communicate. While interacting with a lower realm being, you may attempt a Skill Check to understand the motive behind their words and communicate more effectively with them.

Mage's Disruption

Classes: Mage
Action: Defensive
Reliant Abilities: Intelligence

You can sense the flow of mana, and with quick action can stop another mage in their tracks. Once per encounter as a defensive action, when you see another mage cast a spell you may force them to make a Contested Skill Check against you. If they fail, they are prevented from casting the spell. Other mages use Intelligence for the Contested Skill Check, Bards and Charlatans use Charisma, and Druids and Priests use their Wisdom.

Mage Guild Membership

Classes: Mage
Action: Enduring Feature
Reliant Abilities: Intelligence

This skill marks you as an official member of a mage's guild, granting you access to archives and stores of knowledge. In addition, once per preparation round you may attempt a Skill Check to gain additional aid from the guild in the form of resources or information.

Magic Resistance (10%)

Requirement: Level 6
Classes: Fighter
Action: Defensive
Reliant Abilities: Special

You gain a chance to resist the effects of any spell targeting you. Whenever you would be the target of a spell or prayer, you may attempt a Skill Check to resist its effects, reducing any damage you would take to 0 and ignoring any additional effects of the spell.
Unlike rogues' percentage skills, magic resistance is improved like normal, with each improved level granting an additional 10% chance to resist magical effects.

Manyshot

Classes: Fighter
Action: Offensive
Reliant Abilities: Dexterity

You rain down shots on your enemy from afar. Once per encounter you may make two attacks with a ranged weapon as an offensive action instead of one. Each improved level of manyshot grants you one additional ranged attack each action.

Martyrdom

Requirements: Level 12
Classes: Priest
Action: Offensive
Reliant Abilities: All

Great deeds are not accomplished without sacrifice. You make yours willingly.

You may attempt a Wisdom Skill Check to exchange your life for a great deed performed by your deity. On a success, you die with no chance for returning to life. Make a Fate Roll with a Bonus to determine the impact of your sacrifice. As martyrdom is improved, it may have vast, world-altering effects dependent on the outcome of the Fate Roll.

Medicinal Herbs

Classes: Druid
Action: Exploration
Reliant Abilities: Intelligence, Wisdom

Long before the discovery of magic, druidic circles worked their miracles with what nature provided. You may attempt a Skill Check during an exploration round to heal the wounds of your allies. On a success, you may spend GP to heal a wounded party member. The maximum amount you can heal them is dependent on the amount of GP you use.

- 0-100 GP: Up to 10% of their maximum HP.
- 100-500: Up to 25% of their maximum HP.
- 500-1000: Up to 33% of their maximum HP.
- 1000-5000: Up to 50% of their maximum HP
- 5000-10,000: Up to 100% of their maximum HP

Medicine

Classes: Priest
Action: Utility
Reliant Abilities: Intelligence, Wisdom

Many seminaries teach their followers medicinal practices, so they may act as healers in the world. You may attempt a Skill Check to gain a Bonus towards any Fate Rolls made to heal an injured person.

Meditation

Classes: Druid, Mage, Priest
Action: Preparation
Reliant Abilities: Wisdom

Focus and a calm mind are fundamental to spellcasting. Even late into their lives, many spellcasters still practice meditation.

During a preparation round you may attempt a Skill Check to focus your mind and make it easier to cast spells. On a success, the mana cost to cast any spell is reduced by 1 for the remainder of the day. Each improved level of meditation reduces the mana cost of spells by an additional 1.

Member of the Congregation

Classes: Charlatan
Action: Enduring Feature
Reliant Abilities: Charisma

Consulting with many deities yet devoting yourself to none comes with certain advantages. With a successful Skill Check you are able to seamlessly blend into any religious community and be accepted as a regular member of their congregation.

Misguiding Hand
Classes: Charlatan
Action: Preparation
Reliant Abilities: Charisma

With the proper influence and a little divine push, you are able to interfere with the abilities of other divine magic users attempting to track you.

During a preparation round you may attempt a Skill Check. On a success, any attempts to follow or locate you through divine means fail.

Mobility
Requirements: Level 5
Classes: Fighter, Rogue
Action: Utility
Reliant Abilities: Dexterity

"On the battlefield, only the dead stay still for long."

Whenever you use a different skill with a reliant ability of Dexterity, you may attempt an additional Skill Check at half your ability score. On a success, you gain an additional Bonus towards any Fate Rolls you make with the first skill.

Monster Ecology
Classes: Bard, Druid, Fighter, Mage, Rogue
Action: Exploration
Reliant Abilities: Intelligence

You've encountered a variety of creatures during your travels, and have kept notes on their behaviors. You may attempt a Skill Check to learn the basic details of any monstrous creature you encounter, including its habitat, diet, skills, strengths, and vulnerabilities.

Mortal Protocols
Classes: All
Action: Social
Reliant Abilities: Intelligence

You are familiar with the various peoples and cultures of the world. You may attempt a Skill Check to bridge cultural differences and learn about the customs of a new group of people in order to avoid accidentally offending them or lowering their Attitude towards you.

Mounted Combatant
Classes: Fighter
Action: Utility
Reliant Abilities: Charisma

You expertly guide your mount through the battlefield, maintaining your superior position and reinforcing your allies at a moment's notice. You may attempt a Skill Check on your turn to order your mount to take the reposition action for free. If you succeed, you may still take an Offensive action this round.

Natural Life
Requirements: Level 15
Classes: Druid
Action: Defensive
Reliant Abilities: Wisdom

You draw upon the lifeforce of the flora and fauna surrounding you, restoring your health. As a defensive action, you may attempt a Skill Check to heal yourself. On a success, make a Fate Roll to determine the effect of the healing. The more natural life surrounding you, the larger the Bonus you receive on this roll. Regardless of the Fate Roll, you heal at least 10% of your maximum HP this way.

Nature's Bard

Classes: Druid
Action: Enduring Feature
Reliant Abilities: Charisma

Your deep connection with nature has inspired you to create many works of art, intertwining your magic with each new creation.

Once gained, nature's bard allows you to cast spells using songs like the bard class. Charisma is the reliant ability of any spells cast this way. You still maintain access to your normal Druid spell list and Prayers.

When you gain this skill you immediately gain 5 mana. Every time you gain a level your maximum mana increases by 5. You may use this mana only to cast Variable cost Spells as per the Bard's Musical Spellcasting ability.

Nature's Bloom

Requirements: Level 20
Classes: Druid
Action: Enduring Feature
Reliant Abilities: All

You have tended your bond with nature like a delicate flower, and now it is ready to bloom. Wherever you walk, nature springs to life around you.

Beginning at level 20 you may attempt to learn the Nature's Bloom skill. Once attained, you gain a permanent +5 bonus to all ability scores, up to a maximum of 20. Nature's Bloom may only be trained once and cannot be improved.

Nature's Guidance

Classes: Druid
Action: Preparation, Defensive
Reliant Abilities: Wisdom

You gain knowledge and information through your mystical connection to the environment. During a preparation round you may attempt a Skill Check to learn information about the natural surroundings.

Once per encounter as a defensive action, you may force an opponent to make a Contested Skill Check using their Offense Rating. If they fail, you avoid the attack.

Nonsensical Divine Countenance

Classes: Charlatan
Action: Preparation, Defensive
Reliant Abilities: Charisma

You receive a beatific vision from a random deity, and no one is quite sure why. During a preparation round, you may attempt a Skill Check to receive a direct communication from a random deity in the form of a vision. The vision may be mysterious or its meaning veiled, and you have no way of controlling which deity responds. The Narrator should make a Fate Roll in private to determine the vision you receive.

When used as a defensive action, once per encounter you may attempt a Skill Check to receive the direct help of a random deity. On a success, you are shielded from the next attack that would hit you.

No Quick Deaths

Classes: Fighter
Action: Enduring Feature
Reliant Abilities: Constitution

You continue fighting through your wounds, refusing to go down without a fight. Once per encounter whenever you would be reduced to 0 hp, instead you are reduced to 1. Whenever you improve No Quick Deaths, you may use this feature 1 additional time each encounter.

Open Lock (10%)

Classes: Rogue
Action: Exploration
Reliant Abilities: Special

With a little luck and a lot of patience, you're able to open any lock in front of you. You may attempt a Skill Check at your current percentage to pick a lock that's in your way .

Open lock is is improved by 1% for each successful Skill Check you make while training it, up to a maximum of 100%.

Oracle

Classes: Charlatan, Priest
Action: Enduring Feature

Reliant Abilities: Wisdom

The gods often speak in riddles and half-truths. Only a few are truly capable of understanding their true meaning.

You may attempt to make a Skill Check whenever receiving a message from a divine being. On a success, you gain some understanding of the true intent behind the message.

Organize Alliance

Classes: Bard, Fighter
Action: Social
Reliant Abilities: Charisma

You are an expert at forging alliances between individuals and rallying together a group under a single cause. During a preparation round you may attempt a Skill Check to gather an alliance of individuals together to aid your cause. Make a Fate Roll to determine how large and how driven your group is to follow your orders.

Overwhelming Critical

Classes: Fighter
Action: Enduring Feature
Reliant Abilities: Offense Rating

Whenever you land a critical strike against an enemy, the damage you deal cannot be avoided by a defensive action unless the defender also scores a critical success on their Skill Check.

Parry

Classes: Fighter, Rogue
Action: Defensive

Reliant Abilities: Strength, Dexterity

Once per encounter as a defensive action, you may attempt to make a Skill Check. On a success, you block one incoming weapon attack, reducing any damage dealt by it to 0.

Pathetic Plea
Classes: Charlatan
Action: Defensive
Reliant Abilities: Charisma

You sink to the ground, begging for mercy. Once per encounter you may force an opponent to make a Contested Skill Check using their Offense Rating. If you win the check, they are unable to attack you for the next round.

Penetrate Armor
Classes: Fighter
Action: Enduring Feature
Reliant Abilities: Offense Rating

You skillfully strike at the gaps in your opponent's armor, allowing you to avoid most of their defense. Whenever you attack an armored enemy, you may force them to make a Contested Skill Check with their Offense Rating. If you win this check, the opponent is unable to gain any benefits from their armor against your attacks this round.

Perception
Classes: Any
Action: Utility
Reliant Abilities: Intelligence

You can notice details easily missed by others. You may attempt a Skill Check to gain information about your surroundings or an individual, limited to what you are able to pick up on and notice with your senses.

Perfect Response (10%)
Classes: Rogue
Action: Utility
Reliant Abilities: Special

"It's all about timing…"

You may attempt a Skill Check at your current perfect response percentage. On a success, you know the ideal course of action for a given situation. You may discuss the response with your Narrator, or allow the Narrator to suggest a course of action for you.

Perfect response is improved by 1% for each successful Skill Check you make while training it, up to a maximum of 100%.

Perfect Time Keeping
Classes: Any
Action: Enduring Feature
Reliant Abilities: Intelligence

You are able to keep track of the time in your head, always knowing the time of day even when deep underground.

Persuasion
Classes: All
Action: Utility
Reliant Abilities: Charisma

You may attempt a Skill Check to improve the Attitude of an NPC to try to convince them to aid you. On a success, roll a d10 and increase the NPC's attitude by an amount equal to the result.

Performance
Classes: Bard, Mage
Action: Preparation
Reliant Abilities: Charisma

You perform a magic routine for the public, taking donations from impressed passersby. During a preparation round, you may attempt a Skill Check to perform your routine. On a success, make a Fate Roll and gain an amount of MP equal to twice the result.

Pickpocket (10%)
Classes: Rogue
Action: Utility
Reliant Abilities: Special

You've found people are easily separated from their coin while distracted. It's a little more difficult when they're paying attention, but only a little.

You may attempt a Skill Check with your current pickpocket percentage to steal from a nearby target's pockets.

Pickpocket is improved by 1% for each successful Skill Check you make while training it, to a maximum of 100%.

Planar Ecology
Classes: Bard, Mage, Priest
Action: Exploration

Reliant Abilities: Intelligence

Much remains unknown about how the various realms of existence function. Even those who study the realms thoroughly consider it an imprecise science.
You may attempt a Skill Check to recall a piece of information about the realms of existence beyond the mortal realm.

Planar Patron
Requirements: Level 8
Classes: Mage
Action: Preparation
Reliant Abilities: Charisma

You form a pact with a being from another realm, gaining assistance and information, and occasionally receiving quests. You may only gain Planar Patron once, choosing one extra-planar entity to be your patron when you do so. You should discuss the choice with your Narrator beforehand.

After you gain this skill, you may attempt a Skill Check during a preparation round to make contact with your patron. Your patron may offer you assistance, advice, or bonuses depending on the outcome of a Fate Roll.

Whenever you improve Planar Patron, you may choose to either gain an additional patron, or strengthen your bond to your current patron.

Planar Protocols
Classes: Bard, Mage
Action: Social
Reliant Abilities: Intelligence

Dealing with beings from other realms of existence can be a challenging, and sometimes deadly, affair. You may attempt a Skill Check when interacting with beings from different realms of existence to learn about their etiquette and be able to communicate more effectively with them.

Plan B
Classes: All
Action: Preparation
Reliant Abilities: Intelligence

You spend time studying the area and your party's plan, coming up with contingencies and backups in case things go wrong. During a preparation round, you may attempt a Skill Check. On a success, make a Fate Roll and record the result. The next time a Fate Roll would be made by anyone during the game, use the result you recorded instead of making a new roll.

Prowess
Classes: Fighter
Action: Utility
Reliant Abilities: Intelligence

You have studied the art of combat with a keen mind, outwitting your opponents on the battlefield. Whenever you take an offensive action, you may attempt a Skill Check at half your normal Intelligence score to gain a Bonus towards it.

Quickened Casting
Requirements: Level 12
Classes: Mage
Action: Enduring Feature

Reliant Abilities: Intelligence

You wade into battle, slinging spells to protect your allies and decimate your opponents. During combat rounds, you may cast 2 spells per round instead of just 1. The mana cost of the 2nd spell you cast each round is doubled.

Read Magic Scroll
Classes: Rogue
Action: Utility
Reliant Abilities: Intelligence

Normally only highly educated mages are able to read the complicated formulas scribed onto magic scrolls...normally. You may attempt a Skill Check to read and cast magic from a scroll in your possession. Make a Fate Roll with a Penalty to determine how well you are able to cast it.

Reduce Mana Cost
Requirement: Level 8
Classes: Mage
Action: Enduring Feature
Reliant Abilities: Intelligence, Wisdom

You have learned to manipulate the flow of mana more efficiently, allowing you to cast more spells each day.
Your cost to reduce any mage spell you cast is reduced by 10%, increased by 5% every time you improve this skill up to a maximum of 30%.

Religious Knowledge
Classes: Charlatan, Priest
Action: Exploration
Reliant Abilities: Intelligence

You are well versed in the pantheon of this world and the various religions that worship its deities. Whenever you encounter a religious individual, group, or object, you may attempt a Skill Check to recall information about this particular religion and its customs.

Rending Attack
Classes: Fighter
Action: Utility
Reliant Abilities: Strength

You deal a vicious wound to your enemy, causing continuing damage on subsequent rounds. Once per encounter after you make a successful attack, you may attempt a Skill Check to rend your opponent. On a success, they take half the total damage again at the end of each of the next round. The damaged they take is halved each subsequent round until they are able to heal their wound, or the damage dealt is less than 1.

Resist Fear
Classes: Priest
Action: Defensive
Reliant Abilities: Wisdom

With your deity standing beside you, there is never a need to run in fear. Once per encounter as a defensive action, you may make a Contested Skill Check against the source of one fear spell or ability. If you are successful, it has no effect on you.

Righteous Flame
Classes: Priest
Action: Offensive
Reliant Abilities: Wisdom, Offense Rating

A truly deadly attack in the hands of the most devout followers, you conjure a divine flame powered by your devotion to your deity.

Once per encounter you may summon a righteous flame to attack your enemies. The flame does more damage the closer you are aligned to your deity's tenants. Make a Fate Roll to determine the damage dealt. You gain a larger Bonus to this Fate Roll the more devout of a follower you are to your deity. This Bonus is determined at the Narrator's discretion.

Royal Protocols
Classes: Bard, Charlatan, Mage, Rogue, Priest
Action: Social
Reliant Abilities: Intelligence

The upper echelons of society often operate under a unique set of rules and customs, especially when interacting with kings and queens. Whenever you interact with a noble or a member of royalty, you may attempt a Skill Check to communicate more effectively and without the risk of reducing their Attitude towards you by insulting them.

Sculpt Spell
Requirements: Level 7
Classes: Mage
Action: Enduring Feature
Reliant Abilities: Intelligence

Whenever you cast a spell you may attempt a Skill Check to alter some aspect of the spell. On a successful Skill Check you may:

- Double the area affected by the spell
- Reduce the area affected by the spell to a single target
- Change the damage type of a spell
- Cast the spell without speaking or performing any gestures
- Increase the distance a spell is able to be cast from

The mana cost for your spell is increased by 10 for each effect you choose to add to the spell.

Self-Righteous Flame

Classes: Charlatan
Action: Offensive
Reliant Abilities: Charisma, Offense Rating

True power comes only from within. This you know, and have come to wield that power to bend divine beings to your will.

Once per encounter you can harness your self-righteousness into a flame to attack your enemies. The flame does more damage the higher your own self conviction. Make a Fate Roll to determine the damage dealt. You gain a larger Bonus to this Fate Roll the more you truly believe that your actions are just. This Bonus is determined at the Narrator's discretion.

Sense Faith

Classes: Druid, Priest
Action: Social
Reliant Abilities: Wisdom

You can sense true belief in the hearts of others. You may attempt a Skill Check to detect if an individual is of strong faith, and determine which deity they follow.

Servant of Any Deity

Requirement: Level 5
Classes: Charlatan
Action: Preparation
Reliant Abilities: Charisma

Your willingness to serve any deity has granted you a reputation among the gods, attracting a number of them to call on you for aid. During a preparation round, you may attempt a Skill Check to commune with a deity and be sent on a quest. The deity chosen is random and you can only be on one quest for a deity at a time.

Improved levels of this skill grant more difficult and rewarding quests from deities.

Servant of Nature

Requirement: Level 5
Classes: Druid
Action: Enduring Feature
Reliant Abilities: Wisdom

The spirits of the natural world consider you an ally, granting a boon to your abilities so long as you continue your work.

Any Fate Rolls you make for your druidic Prayers and abilities in a wooded area gain a Bonus. You lose these abilities if you stop following your druidic tenants, at the Narrator's discretion.

Shadow of the Great Tree

Requirements: Level 10
Classes: Druid
Action: Exploration
Reliant Abilities: Wisdom

You call upon the spirit of the great tree to grant shade and protection to you and your allies. Once per encounter you may attempt a Skill Check to summon a magical shadow of the great tree. On a success, the sun is blocked by a shadow, granting shade in a large area around you. You and your allies gain a Bonus to any attempt to hide while in the shade.

Shield Bash

Classes: Fighter
Action: Enduring Feature
Reliant Abilities: Offense Rating

You turn your shield into a fearsome melee weapon, defending yourself and striking at opponents in the same fluid motion. Whenever you make an Offensive action using a weapon, you may use your shield instead. When you do so, you may make an extra defensive action during that round.

Shot on the Run

Classes: Fighter
Action: Utility
Reliant Abilities: Dexterity, Wisdom

Once per encounter, you may attempt a Skill Check to be able to move and make an attack as part of the same offensive action during this turn. On a success, you may use an Offensive Skill and take the reposition action for free on this turn. If you fail the Skill Check, your action for the turn is used and you do not gain the benefits from this Skill.

Silent Prayer

Requirements: Level 6
Classes: Charlatan, Druid, Priest
Action: Enduring Feature
Reliant Abilities: Wisdom

You are able to cast spells silently and without noticeable hand gestures. You are harder to notice while casting a spell, and may still cast even if you are unable to speak or move.

Simony

Classes: Charlatan
Action: Enduring Feature
Reliant Abilities: Charisma

"Those who say you can't buy your way into heaven simply don't have enough money."

You may donate MP to a deity in exchange for blessings, spells, protection, and forgiveness. The cost of these bonuses are unknown to you and dependent on the outcome of a Fate Roll.

Sleight of Hand

Classes: Bard, Mage, Rogue
Action: Utility
Reliant Abilities: Dexterity
With skillful deception and a practiced quickness, you pull off everything from simple magic tricks to expert pickpocketing. You may attempt a Skill Check to perform small bits of practical magic or card tricks.

In addition, as a free action you may attempt a Skill Check at half your normal Dexterity score to gain a Bonus towards another skill you are using which requires manual dexterity.

Slippery Mind

Classes: All
Action: Enduring Feature
Reliant Abilities: Wisdom

Your thoughts are harder to detect and anyone who seeks to connect with your mind might find themselves lost in it. Whenever anyone seeks to connect telepathically with your mind, they must make a Fate Roll with a Penalty to determine if they are able to make sense of your thoughts.

In addition, once per encounter as a defensive action you may attempt a Skill Check to defend yourself from any telepathic spells or abilities. Make a Contested Skill Check against the target's Intelligence. If you succeed, the spell has no effect on you.

Skillful

Classes: All
Action: Enduring Feature
Reliant Abilities: All

You are a quick learner, gaining new abilities with exceptional aptitude. Whenever you level up you may gain 1 additional new skill.

Spellcasting Harrier

Classes: Fighter
Action: Defensive
Reliant Abilities: Charisma

Using insults, threats, and distractions, you break a spellcaster's concentration, preventing them from casting a spell. Once per encounter as a defensive action, when a spellcaster you can see attempts to cast a spell, you may force them to make a Contested Skill Check with their Wisdom. If you win the check, the spellcaster does not spend any mana and is prevented from casting the spell.

Spellcrafting

Requirements: Level 5
Classes: Mage
Action: Preparation
Reliant Abilities: Intelligence, Wisdom
Through experimenting with various alignments of magical runes you are able to create spells of your very own design. During a preparation round you may attempt a Skill Check to begin the process of creating a new spell. On a success, spend an amount of gathering points and make a Fate Roll to determine the progress you make.
Spells crafted by this method must be of a level you are able to cast. You should work with your Narrator to determine how the spell specifically functions in your game.

Spring Attack

Classes: Fighter
Action: Offensive
Reliant Abilities: Dexterity, Offense Rating

You leap forward suddenly, catching your opponent off guard. Once per encounter you may attempt a Skill Check to attack an enemy outside your normal reach. On a success, you close the distance between yourself and the enemy and make a Fate Roll to deal damage.

Stealth (10%)
Classes: Rogue
Action: Exploration
Reliant Abilities: Special

You meld into the shadows, hiding yourself from view and effectively becoming invisible. You may attempt a Skill Check at your current stealth percentage to become hidden. If you succeed, you are considered invisible and cannot be spotted by ordinary means.
Stealth is improved by 1% for each successful Skill Check you make while training it, up to a maximum of 100%.

Storm of Throws
Requirements: Dual Wielding
Classes: Fighter
Action: Offensive
Reliant Abilities: Strength, Offense Rating

You overwhelm your opponents with a torrent of thrown weapons. Once per encounter you may attempt a Skill Check. On a success, you may make 1 additional thrown weapon attack with each hand during this round of combat, up to a maximum of 4 total attacks.

Storytelling
Classes: Bard
Action: Social
Reliant Abilities: Charisma

Enthralling a crowd with little more than your words alone is a feat few are capable of. You may attempt a Skill Check to tell a story to entertain a crowd. When used during a preparation round, make a Fate Roll to determine how much MP you are able to make from your craft.

Stunning Blow
Classes: Fighter
Action: Offensive
Reliant Abilities: Offense Rating

You strike an opponent's vulnerable spot, reducing your damage but incapacitating them temporarily. Once per encounter you may attempt a Skill Check to stun an opponent for 1 round, preventing them from taking any actions but dealing no damage with your attack.

Swarm of Arrows
Requirements: Manyshot
Classes: Fighter
Action: Enduring Feature
Reliant Abilities: Dexterity, Offense Rating

Once per encounter when you use the manyshot skill, you may choose to forgo any additional attacks and turn the action into an area of effect attack, making one roll for the entire action instead of individual rolls for each opponent.

Swimming

Classes: All
Action: Utility
Reliant Abilities: Strength, Constitution

You never know where your adventures might lead. One minute you're on a bridge, then for a few seconds you're falling, and the next thing you know you're submerged in water being swept down a river.

You may attempt a Skill Check to be able to tread water or swim even in harsh conditions. You suffer a Penalty to this check if you are wearing armor or carrying heavy equipment.

Tearful Confession

Classes: Charlatan
Action: Defensive
Reliant Abilities: Charisma

You make a heartfelt admission of your guilt, gaining the trust of those around you.
Once per encounter you may attempt a Skill Check to make a tearful confession.
During a social encounter, success makes those who witness you more likely to trust you in the future, improving their Attitude towards you.
During a combat encounter, a success makes all enemies unable to target you with attacks for the next round.

Temple Sigil

Classes: Priest
Action: Enduring Feature
Reliant Abilities: Wisdom, Charisma

You bear the official sigil of your deity's temple and are marked as an official member of the community. You gain access to shelter and support whenever you visit a temple dedicated to your god.

Improved levels of Temple Sigil represent a higher ranking within the temple's leadership.

Thaumaturgy

Classes: Mage
Action: Preparation
Reliant Abilities: Intelligence, Wisdom

During a preparation round you may attempt a Skill Check in order to spend gathering points to cast a spell instead of mana.

Thieves Guild Membership

Classes: Bard, Rogue
Action: Enduring Feature
Reliant Abilities: Charisma

You are a trusted member of one of the world's many underworld operations.
As a member of a thieves guild, you gain access to any secret hideouts or facilities operated by your guild, as well as any of the guild's business operations. In addition, you may occasionally receive aid, assistance, or jobs from the guild.

Timeslip

Requirements: Level 10
Classes: All
Action: Enduring Feature
Reliant Abilities: All

You gain immunity from any effects causing time to stop for you. Spells targeting an area may still affect other individuals within that area.

Trip Attack
Classes: Fighter, Rogue
Action: Offensive
Reliant Abilities: Dexterity, Offense Rating

Once per encounter as an offensive action, you may attempt a Skill Check to knock an opponent off their feet. On a success, you deal no damage but the target is knocked prone.

Trust Me, I Know a Guy
Classes: Bard, Rogue
Action: Preparation
Reliant Abilities: Charisma

You know just the right person to get a certain job done, but whether they'll accept or not is a different story. During a preparation round you may attempt a Skill Check. On a success, you recall a contact nearby able to help with a specific job.

Underworld Connection
Classes: Rogue
Action: Preparation
Reliant Abilities: Charisma
You are familiar with many of the underworld figures in the area, and a few of them might even still be willing to help you. During a preparation round you may attempt a Skill Check. On a success, you know an individual connected with this area's underworld that may be willing to help you.

Undying Faith
Requirements: Level 15
Classes: Priest
Action: Enduring Feature
Reliant Abilities: Wisdom

Your belief in your deity allows you to push your body past its normal limits. Once per encounter, when you would be dealt a lethal blow, instead you are reduced to 1 HP.

In addition, any prayers you cast during an encounter continue past your death, only fading once your allies are safe from danger.

Unholy Rebuke
Classes: Priest
Action: Offensive
Reliant Abilities: Charisma

You wield the dark energies of your deity, commanding any undead nearby to obey your commands. Once per encounter as an offensive action, you may attempt a Skill Check. On a success, any lesser undead in the area obey your commands.

Unnoticeable
Classes: Bard, Druid, Rogue
Action: Exploration
Reliant Abilities: Dexterity, Wisdom
You can slip into the shadows hiding yourself from view. You can stand amongst a crowd and yet no one will recognize you. You can survey a palace guard's patrol without raising any suspicion.

On a successful Skill Check, you go unnoticed by most creatures that do not have any special senses. Any creature attempting to spot you must succeed on a Contested Skill Check with their Wisdom against either your Dexterity or Wisdom (your choice).

Upper Realm Connection

Requirements: Level 6
Classes: Charlatan, Mage, Priest
Action: Preparation
Reliant Abilities: Charisma

Through your commune with the upper realms of existence you have made acquaintances which you may periodically call upon for aid. During a preparation round you may attempt a Skill Check. On a success, you contact a being of the upper realms to ask for knowledge or aid.

Upper Realm Travel

Requirements: Level 11
Classes: Charlatan, Priest
Action: Preparation
Reliant Abilities: Charisma

You transport yourself and your party to the upper realms of existence, allowing you to communicate more directly with your divine patrons. Once per month during a preparation round, you may attempt a Skill Check to gain access to the upper realms. Make a Fate Roll to determine which deity responds and where on the upper realms you appear.

Upper Realm Protocols

Classes: All
Action: Social
Reliant Abilities: Charisma

The upper realms are a strange place, full of powerful divine beings both separated from and intimately connected to the mortal realms. Whenever you are dealing with beings from the upper realms you may attempt a Skill Check. On a success, you understand the nuances and customs of the upper realms and are able to communicate more effectively.

Walk in Like I Own the Place

Classes: Bard, Rogue
Action: Utility
Reliant Abilities: Charisma

"The trick is to just act like you belong." When you enter a new location you may attempt a Skill Check. On a success, people treat you like you belong until you do something to reveal yourself.

Whirlwind Attack

Classes: Fighter
Action: Offensive
Reliant Abilities: Offense Rating

Even while surrounded by enemies you are a force to be reckoned with. Once per encounter as an offensive action, you may attempt an attack against all enemies within your reach. Make only 1 attack roll and apply it to each enemy.

Woodland Ecology

Classes: Bard, Druid, Fighter, Rogue
Action: Exploration
Reliant Abilities: Int

You may attempt a Skill Check to recall a useful piece of information regarding the forests or woodlands, including any local flora and fauna and major geographical features of this area.

Wrestler

Classes: Fighter
Action: Offensive
Reliant Abilities: Strength, Dexterity

In the past your enemies have thought you defenseless without your weapon. They were wrong.

As an offensive action, you may force an opponent to make a Contested Skill Check. Both you and your opponent may select between Strength or Dexterity for the check. If you are successful, you tie up your opponent in a grapple, preventing them from moving or taking other complex actions. On subsequent rounds, as long as the opponent has not escaped your grapple, you may attempt a Skill Check to perform dynamic unarmed moves. Opponents may attempt another Contested Skill Check on each of their turns to attempt to break free.

Horus and his Little Buddy
(though to be perfectly honest I'm not sure which is which)

Chapter 12: Spellcasting

Certain classes gain access to powerful magical abilities in the form of spellcasting. While casting a spell or a prayer, spellcasters open themselves up to dangerous energies from other realms of existence, acting as a conduit for those energies to enter the mortal realm.

Mages and Bards gain 9 mana / level to spend in the casting of spells. In order to replenish their reserve of mana, spellcasters must have a good rest. This typically occurs while they sleep, so periods of little rest can be especially taxing for these spellcasters.

Charlatans, Druids, and Priests cast their spells differently. Rather than developing their own source of mana, their spells are granted to them by the spirits of nature for Druids, their deity for Priests, and multiple deities for Charlatans. The frequency these classes may cast a specific spell is listed under the spell's description in the next chapter.

Spells are inherently different from Skills in that they require no Skill Checks to be cast successfully. Spells are still subject to Fate Rolls, and at the discretion of the Narrator may be limited to use inside or out of combat rounds.

An Imprecise Science

Even by the most skilled spellcasters, magic isn't considered a precise science. Mages are often dealing with extremely potent energies from other realms of existence, while other spellcasters are in constant negotiation with their deity for access to their powers.

To represent this in the game, Spells are generally given less specific descriptions of their effects than Skills. Similar to how players are encouraged to be creative in their application of Skills, spellcasters must use their creativity to leverage their Spells in the most powerful ways.

While you are free to set the limits and mechanics of specific Spells as the Narrator in your game and have the final say in these matters, it is recommended you allow your players to suggest the effects of the Spell, and make a Fate Roll to determine how well those effects play out for their character. A low Fate Roll may mean the Spell doesn't have quite the effect the spellcaster intended, or they do not have as much control of it as they thought.

As with Skills, Spells are intended to represent narrative options the characters possess to overcome obstacles in their path, rather than define a specific set of mechanics in the game.

Learning New Spells

Spellcasters may spend their time during a preparation round studying or researching a new spell from their spell list.

Similar to training a new Skill, you must succeed in a series of Skill Checks to permanently add the spell to your repertoire.

The reliant abilities for all spells are considered to be Intelligence and Wisdom. Therefore, you must make 5 successful Intelligence and 5 successful Wisdom Skill Checks to gain access to the new spell.

If you do not succeed on every Skill Check on your first attempt, record any successes you have made on your character sheet, and apply those towards your next attempt at learning the spell.

Charlatans, Druids, and Priests may spend a Preparation round attempting to increase the frequency they can use one of their Prayers instead of learning a new one. Make all Skill Checks listed above but instead of adding a new Prayer to your list, you gain one additional use of a Prayer you already know.

For Example: A Priest could attempt to train their *Bless* Prayer. If they succeed all 5 Intelligence and 5 Wisdom Skill Checks, they would be able to use *Bless* 2/day instead of only once.

Variable Cost Spells

Most Mage spells have a mana cost listed in their description, though some spells' mana costs are left indeterminate. These are flexible spells a spellcaster is able to pour as much of their mana reserve as they like into. The more mana used in the casting of the spell, the greater the effect.
(*Note:* In a Bard's case, any spell they cast is considered to be a variable cost spell.)

While your Narrator is free to determine the specific mechanics of variable cost spells, a good rule to follow is to make a Fate Roll and add a Bonus equal to the amount of Mana used in the Spell's casting to determine its effects. You may use the table below as a basis for the scale of effects capable using different amounts of Mana.

Mana Used	Spell Effects
1	Trivial effect on a single person
5	Moderate effect on a single person
9	Significant effect on a single person
20	Moderate effect on a small group
30	Significant effect on a small group
40	Moderate effect on a general area or fantastic effect on a single person
50	Significant effect on a general area
75	Minor reality shaping effects
100+	Near mastery over Spell's effects

Variable cost spells are listed as "Var." in the Mage's Spell list.

Creating New Spells

Similar to Skills, it is quite easy to create new Spells by following the examples in the next chapter. You should work with your Narrator to determine the balance of Mana cost frequency with the spell's effects in the game.

If a spellcaster is trying to create a new spell in the moment, you can handle it as a variable cost spell with a Fate Roll to determine how well they can improvise the new spell. In this case, a penalty to the Fate Roll may be warranted depending on the situation.

The frequency they may cast their spells with is listed instead of the mana cost.

Reading the Spell List

The following chapter contains a list of spells readily available to your spellcasters. Spells are broken down into the level of a particular spellcasting class you need to be in order to learn that spell.

Spell Name	Cost/Frequency	Description

As you gain levels, you can learn more powerful Spells and Prayers. The Spell lists in the next chapter list the minimum level of that spellcasting class you must be to learn those new Spells.

Certain spells represent schools of study and may be improved as you level up. Additional levels of these Spells are listed on the spell list at later class levels and have a number listed after the spell name. Improvements in these Spells represent a greater mastery or understanding of the general principle of magic they represent. Charlatans, Druids, and Priests cast their spells without mana, on a per diem basis.

Archmage Immense Numbers

Chapter 13: Spell Lists

Spell List

Level 1:

Spell Name	Mana Cost	Description
Amplify Entertainment	3	Greatly improve the Attitudes of anyone currently having a good time
Cryomancy	6	Minor control over the temperature of an area, can freeze liquids
Divination	9	Gain information and visions from mystical sources
Genetic Manipulation	5	Alter a creature on a fundamental level to change its strengths and weaknesses
Ironic Escape	9	Magically remove you and your allies from one bad situation only to land in an equally bad situation
Likable Rapport	5	Sway NPCs' Attitude towards you more effectively
Magical Gag	3	Play small, harmless pranks on people to annoy or distract them
Magic Tricks	Var	Perform minor magic tricks and illusions
Pyromancy	6	Minor control of fire and flame
Raining Disgust	Var	Conjure a cloud that rains down putrid smelling water and filth in an area
Summoning	9	Conjure a Minion level ally from another realm to aid you
Technomancy	5	Control an ordinary or magical device near you
Telekinesis	8	Move one small object with your mind
Warding	4	Place a protective ward on an individual or area, alerting you when something is wrong

Level 2:

Spell Name	Mana Cost	Description
Aromatic Cloud	10	The next spell you casts becomes an aroma, affecting anyone who smells it
Cryomancy 2	14	Greater control over temperature, can make a room freezing cold
Dazzle	8	Conjure a display of color and lights to distract or draw attention

Find Portal	10	Locate hidden portals to other realms of existence, cannot create new portals
Heartfelt Gift	15	Instantly summon an ordinary item worth 100MP or less that one individual would sincerely love receiving
Mechanical Minion	10	Conjure a small, mechanical companion capable of following simple orders
Pyromancy 2	14	Greater control over flames, can start a fire with magic alone
Rejuvenating Nap	12	Put someone to sleep for 15 minutes to restore a part of their health and mana
Taste It	5	Make an individual experience their current mental and emotional state as a flavor
Technomancy 2	12	Greater control over devices near you
Telekinesis 2	15	Move heavier objects with greater control

Level 3:

Spell Name	Mana Cost	Description
Antimagic field	Var	Counter another magical effect or spell
Drain Luck	Var	The target takes a Penalty to the next Fate Roll they make and you gain an equal Bonus to your next Fate Roll.
Genetic Manipulation 2	15	Change a creature in minor physical ways to grant it small abilities
Haste	22	Double your actions for 3 rounds
Put Pocket	15	Magically transfer an ordinary item to the target's pocket
Sharpen	Var	Magically grant a Bonus to a physical or mental attack
Summon 2	20	Stronger allies come to your aid
Two for One	Var	Double the effects of a selected action

Level 4:

Spell Name	Mana Cost	Description
Banishing	32	Send a creature back to its home realm of existence
Cryomancy 3	30	Freeze the ground in an area or conjure ice shards
Invisibility	20	Shroud a creature in magic to make them invisible
Portal Manipulation	Var	Expand, shrink, or close already existing portals
Pyromancy 3	30	Conjure blasts of fire to attack your enemies
Sting	Var	Mimic the sting of an insect or arachnid
Summon 3	30	Summon multiple creatures to aid you
Technomancy 3	25	Conjure simple devices magically
Telekinesis 3	26	Move objects up to 50 pounds with your mind
Three for One	Var	Triple the effects of a selected action
Wall	Var	Permanently conjure a solid wall no taller than a single story building.
Warding 2	20	Place a protective ward on an individual, protecting them against damage, or on area to keep out intruders

Level 5:

Spell Name	Mana Cost	Description
Bestow Skill	Var	Grant one of your skills to an ally temporarily
Divination 2	45	Gain more detailed information or attempt to locate objects remotely
Genetic Manipulation 3	35	Adapt a creature to be able to survive in different environments, give creatures wings, fins, burrowing claws, etc
Hive Mind	30	Magically link your party's minds together so you may communicate telepathically
Time Harm	30	Undo any healing effects a creature has recently received
Stop Time	45	Stop 1 target in time for a brief period

Level 6:

Spell Name	Mana Cost	Description
Cryomancy 4	50	Freeze a larger area, create objects from ice
Four for One	Var	Quadruple the effects of a selected action
Pyromancy 4	50	Easily control raging fires, manipulate a fire's shape
Restoration	54	Restore 1 being to the physical state they were in 1 hour ago, including any Health Points and Mana
Summoning 4	40	Attempt to summon a common individual from another realm, they may act of their own volition and are not necessarily loyal to you
Technomancy 4	50	Conjure more complex devices to aid your adventures
Telekinesis 4	50	Move objects up to 100 pounds and perform complex actions

Level 7:

Spell Name	Mana Cost	Description
Divination 3	50	Search for the location of individuals in the same realm as you
Genetic Manipulation 4	55	Make significant changes to a creature's body and grant it stronger abilities
Summoning 5	60	Summon a warrior or noble from another realm of existence, they may act of their own volition and are not necessarily loyal to you, and may hold their summoning against you.
Time Heal	70	Rewind time a short amount for 1 individual, healing any wounds they have received
Time Lock	Var	Lock a period of time in place and allow you to replay it, potentially changing the outcome of events

Level 8:

Spell Name	Mana Cost	Description
Chronomancy 1	Var	Pause, rewind, and speed-up time in a small area around you.
Genetic Manipulation 5	65	Change the body size and structure of a creature or the organization of its limbs.

Puppet Strings	70	Remotely control an opponent's movements through magical strings
Read Timeline	Var	See into the past, present, and future of an object or person
Summoning 6	70	Summon a powerful being from another realm, they may act of their own volition and are not necessarily loyal to you, and may hold their summoning against you.
Transmute Metal	Var	Change 1 type of metal into another
Warding 3	50	Place a powerful ward on a single person or create a defensive bubble of protection.

Level 9:

Spell Name	Mana Cost	Description
Cryomancy 5	70	Freeze even larger area, create complex objects and structures from ice
Pyromancy 5	70	Create walls of flame and enhance allies' weapons with flaming properties
Swarm	55	Temporarily transform your body into a swarm of smaller creatures
Technomancy 5	70	Create devices capable of helping your allies in battle
Telekinesis 5	65	Move multiple objects or another creature with your mind

Level 10:

Spell Name	Mana Cost	Description
Butterfly Effect	Var	Take a small action now in hopes it will lead to a much larger outcome in the future
Divination 4	60	Locate objects and individuals across realms of existence
Fusion	Var	Take 2 willing beings and fuse them into a new, unique entity
Genetic Manipulation 6	85	Accelerate the evolutionary path of a creature to alter its physical appearance and abilities greatly

Level 12:

Spell Name	Mana Cost	Description
Chronomancy 2	110	Control the flow of time in a larger area around you.
Clean Timeline	100	Remove any effects of time travel from 1 individual's timeline and reset it to how it was before any chronomancy was done.
Cryomancy 6	110	Create and manipulate structures of ice with ease
Pyromancy 6	110	Control fire over widespread areas
Technomancy 6	110	Conjure complex technology from a point in the future of your timeline
Telekinesis 6	100	Move multiple individuals at the same time with your mind
Warding 4	90	Place a ward to defend against most ordinary attacks

Level 18:

Spell Name	Mana Cost	Description
Chronomancy 3	150	Partial mastery over the flow of time
Cryomancy 7	125	Mastery over cold and ice
Pyromancy 7	125	Mastery over fire and flame
Speed Destiny	144	Jump forward in your own timeline to the next major event, you may not alter any period of time in between when you begin this jump and when you land.
Technomancy 7	125	Mastery over technology
Telekinesis 7	125	Mastery of telekinetic powers

Prayer List

Level 1

Spell Name	Frequency	Description
Bless	1 / day	Grant an ally divine favor on their actions, they gain a Bonus towards Fate Rolls or Skill Checks (your choice)
Hallowed Ground	1 / week	Bless the ground in a small area around you, allies are protected from attacks from undead and evil sources within this area.
Hex	1 / day	Inflict a hex on an enemy, granting a Penalty towards any Fate Rolls
Holy Aroma	1 / day	Transform another spell or ability into an aroma, affecting all who smell it.
Holy Undead	1 / day	Stop undead creatures from advancing towards you
Lesser Healing	3 / day	Heal up to 25% of an ally's maximum HP
Red Hand of the Killer	1 / month	Mark someone who has committed a terrible deed with scarlet red hands
Sign of Power	1 / day	Perform a minor miracle as a demonstration of your deity's power
Tongues of People and Angels	1/ day	Gain the ability to speak any language

Level 2:

Spell Name	Frequency	Description
Blessed Sleep	1 / day	Put someone into a deep sleep, healing both their physical and spiritual wounds
Commune with Holy Text	At will	Instantly absorb the information found without a religious text (Priest only)
Contact Entity	1 / day	Reach out to beings in other realms of existence
Detect Subterfuge	1 / day	Detect individuals attempting to lie or hide the truth
Fae Messenger	1 / day	Summon a fae creature to deliver a message (Druid only)
Leap of Faith	3 / day	Dramatically increase the distance you or an ally can jump
Moderate Healing	1 / day	Heal up to 50% of an ally's maximum HP.
Summon Planar Ally	1 / week	Summon a weaker being from the upper or lower

		realms to assist you
Truth Will Set You Free	1 / week	Bind a known liar to a single are until they tell the truth

Level 3:

Spell Name	Frequency	Description
Astral Projection	1 / week	Send your soul out of your body to commune with the upper or lower realms
Aura of Blessed Silence	1 / day	Prevent all sound and mental attacks within an area, including possessions
Cornucopia	3 / week	Summon a feast capable of feeding a large number of people
Improved Healing	1 / 2 days	Heal up to 75% of an ally's maximum HP
Hide From Enemies	1 / week	Remain undetected as long as you are stationary and praying
Holy Binding	1 / month	Bind a summoned creature to a holy site
Sacramental Seal	1 / day	Lock a scroll or book so that it may only be opened under specific holy rites
Salvage	1 / week	Raise an object lost under the sea or buried in the earth for no more than 1 week
Summon Hellfire	1 / week	Conjure unholy flames that burn both body and soul
Zone of Chaos/Order	1 / day	Protect a zone against beings of chaos or order (your choice)

Level 4:

Spell Name	Frequency	Description
Banishing	1 / day	Send a creature back to its home realm of existence
Breath of Life	No limit	Give up your own Health Points to heal an ally for an equal amount
Call of the Fae	1 / day	Call all nearby fae creatures to your area (Druid only)
Control Hellfire	1 / day	Gain control over hellfire as if casting the Pyromancy spell
Mercy	1 / day	Prevent a creature from feeling pain

Oracle	1 / month	Consult with your deity about past or future events
Spirit Form	1 / week	Send your soul to the spiritual realm to commune with beings there

Level 5:

Spell Name	Frequency	Description
Angelic Aspect 1	1 / week	Summon a lesser aspect of your deity, such as a holy weapon or angelic messenger
Discern Location	1 / week	Learn the location of a specific object or person
Realm Adaptation	1 / day	Adapt to the environment of another realm
Summon Planar Ally 2	1 / week	Summon a stronger ally from the upper or lower realms to aid you
Transport via Holy Site	1 / day	Instantly travel between two locations of significant important to your religion

Level 6:

Spell Name	Frequency	Description
Absolution	1 / week	Grant someone relief from guilt and free them of any sins they have committed towards your deity
Create Peace	1 / year	End all conflict for 1 hour over a large area
Death to the Undead	1 / week	Destroy an undead creature permanently with a Contested Skill Check
Divine Inspiration	1 / week	Gain divine guidance or knowledge from your deity
Stunning Word of the Divine	1 / 3 days	Stun a small group of enemies for a round with the profound words of your deity

Level 7:

Spell Name	Frequency	Description
Return to Life	1 / month	Restore life to an individual who has recently passed
Soul Binding	1 / month	Bind an entity to the physical body it is currently possessing
Superior Healing	1 / 3 days	Fully restore the health of an ally
Tree of Life 1	1 / month	Summon a magical tree with healing fruit

Level 8:

Spell Name	Frequency	Description
Angelic Aspect 2	1 / month	Summon a stronger aspect of your deity
Clear Contingencies	1 / day	Attempt to disable any magical contingencies of an enemy spellcaster with a Contested Skill Check
Control Weather	1 / month	Gain control over the weather in a large area around you
Dimensional Lock	1 / day	Prevent beings from entering or leaving your realm in a small area around you
Holy Temple	1 / year	Summon a permanent temple dedicated to your deity on an open patch of land
Planar Adaptation 2	1 / week	Adapt you and your allies to the environment of other realms
Rock Band of the Angels	1 / month	A band of angels inspires you and your allies
Spell Crash	1 / 3 days	Counter up to a 7th level spell and prevent its casting
Summon Planar Ally 3	1 / month	Summon an angel or demon to assist you

Level 9:

Spell Name	Frequency	Description
Escape the Cage	1 / week	Magically escape from any captivity or bonds
Miracle	1 / year	Your deity grants you a large favor
Return to Life 2	1 / year	Resurrect a large number of individuals who have passed within the last day
Vengeful Gaze	1 / month	Levy the power of your deity on an individual and make them relive their most terrible deeds
Word of Exorcism	1 / month	Instantly free a person from possession by a being from a different realm

Level 12:

Spell Name	Frequency	Description
Banishing 2	1 / year	Banish a creature to a realm other than it's home realm

Disenchant Item	1 / month	Remove the magical effects of an item, both harmful and helpful
Last Day of the Witch	1 / year	Force Mages and Bards to make a Contested Skill Check in order to cast any magic over a large area
Tree of Life 2	1 / year	Summon a small grove of magical trees with healing fruit

Level 15:

Spell Name	Frequency	Description
Eternalize	1 / year	Make the effects of a spell permanent
Holy Army	1 / year	The next spell you cast affects up to 300 individuals
Holy Disjunction	1 / Month	Suppress the effects of all magical items and abilities of your target and reduce their mana to 0.
True Death	1 / year	Make it so an individual cannot be resurrected or brought back to life by any means

Level 18:

Spell Name	Frequency	Description
Ascension	Once	Elevate a being to a higher state of existence
Summon Holy Artifact	Once	Conjure a unique artifact relating to your deity

Chapter 14: Appendices

Appendix A: Quick Start Guide

Listen, we get it. Whether you're a veteran TTRPG player or you'd rather learn the game by playing it than reading through the past hundred or so pages, we've prepared a quick start guide so you can jump right in and begin telling stories.[23]

Before you Play

Start by selecting 1 player at the table to be the Narrator. This player is responsible for running the game as well as describing the action, playing any NPCs, and interpreting Fate Rolls. It is recommended that this player has some experience running other TTRPGs.

Instead of having a full Session 0, which is described in **Chapter 9**, you should have a short conversation about the game you will all be playing. Discuss the tone, genre, and style, as well as any topics you would like excluded from the game. Your goal here is to make sure everyone is on the same page and everyone's expectations have been made clear. As a base safety tool, we recommend that a player at the table raise their fist if they are uncomfortable and need the Narrator to progress the scene.

Go around the table and have each player contribute 1 fact about the world of your game. It can be anything as minor or as grand as the player wishes - from "There is an evil immortal king who rules a kingdom in the north," to "The grass here is purple."

Character Creation
The other players at the table will play the Characters. Give your character a name and describe what they look like. Don't worry! Your character's physical appearance has no mechanical impact in the game unless you want it to. Be sure to keep track of your character's details on a character sheet or a separate piece of paper!

Characters have 6 **Attributes** that describe their physical and mental traits and are used to make Skill Checks. These attributes are:
- Strength - physical power
- Dexterity - agility, flexibility
- Constitution - fortitude, toughness
- Intelligence - mental acuity
- Wisdom - judgment, perception
- Charisma - likeability, eloquence

To determine your attribute scores, roll a 20-sided die 8 times. Remove the 2 lowest results and record the remaining numbers in any order you wish to your attributes on your character sheet.

Your character in the NU can be whatever you want it to be, but keep in mind the other players at your table. Be sure to make a character that will fit with the rest of the party in the story.

Now you're just about ready to begin playing! Discuss with your Narrator what, if any, starting equipment your characters may have at their disposal. Don't worry about choosing a Class or Skills for now. The Quick Start Guide is about getting a sense of how the Skill Check and Fate Roll systems. You can always add the rest of the

---

[23] Don't worry, it won't hurt the writer's feelings *too* much

details to your character sheet later if your party wants to continue this story.

Telling the Story

The NU is a storytelling game. As you play, the Narrator will begin telling the story by describing the setting and any action occurring around the party. Characters may interact with the story as they wish, changing the narrative with their actions.

Skill Checks

Whenever a character attempts an action, the Narrator will tell them to make a **Skill Check** involving 1 or more of your attributes. The attributes chosen should reflect the abilities needed to accomplish the action.

For example: Solving a complicated equation may require Intelligence, while lifting a heavy object requires Strength.

For more complicated actions, you may be required to perform more than 1 Skill Check to achieve your goal. For instance, crafting an herbal remedy out of plants you foraged may require both an Intelligence and a Wisdom Skill Check.

To make a Skill Check, roll a 20-sided die for each attribute involved. The NU uses a **Roll-Under System**, meaning a success is any outcome on the die *less than or equal to* your current attribute score, meaning your character completes the action they were attempting.

Fate Rolls

When an action has a big impact on the narrative of the story, a **Fate Roll** is required to determine the narrative impact of that action.

Fate Rolls help the Narrator determine what happens next after a character performs an action that has consequences to the progression of the story. They also ensure the Narrator remains an equal player at the table, telling a story *with* the other players rather than *to* them. Fate Rolls are always made with a d100 (or 2d10s).

- A high roll means the action has a positive outcome in favor of the party
- A low roll means this action has negative consequences or leads to further difficulty.
- Rolls towards the middle of the spectrum is a mixed success and presents opportunities for the party to move the story in their favor, but at an increased cost or risk.
- No matter the outcome, *the story always moves forward.*

It is important to remember that a Fate Roll does not impact the success of the action, merely the impact the action has on the narrative.

For example: If a character is trying to open a locked drawer and they succeed on their Skill Check to do so, the drawer should open for them either way. What they find inside the drawer may rely on a Fate Roll - a high roll might give them a vital clue to a mystery they are solving, while a low roll may give them a false lead or add further confusion to their quest.

Combat

Should a situation arise where combat is unavoidable, the following rules will help you keep track of the battle.

- It is recommended to track your Health Points as a percentage out of

100 for now. Other options are presented in **Chapter 8.**

- Opposing sides act together as a team on their turn. To determine which team goes first, every combatant rolls a d20. The highest overall roll wins first action for their team.
- Each combatant may take 1 action on each of their turns.
- Combatants should describe their action and make any Skill Checks requested by the Narrator.
- On a successful Skill Check, make a Fate Roll and deal damage equal to that percentage of the enemy's Health Points.
- Whenever you are hit by an attack, you may give up your action for your next turn to attempt to defend yourself using a Skill Check.
- If an attack is successfully defended, both the attacker and defender roll a d100. Subtract the defender's result from the attacker's and deal any remaining damage to the defender. If the defender rolls higher than the attacker, the attack deals no damage.
- When a combatant is reduced to 0 HP, or is dealt more than 80% of the health in a single attack, they are knocked out and removed from combat.

Continuing Your Story

If you wish to continue the story with your current characters and Narrator, it is quite simple to pick up the rest of the system now that you know the basics!

Choose a class for each of your characters, as well as your skills from the skill list in

Chapter 11. If you don't see a skill listed your group has been using, feel free to add it yourself using the template found in **Chapter 10!**

Now you're ready to begin playing games in the Narrative Universe[24]!

Bertie the Death Bard, Son of Hades

The following page contains a Sample NU character sheet you can print for your games. Visit the ONU Discord for a Fillable PDF version!

---

[24] And, you know, hopefully read the rest of this book. We put a lot of work into it.

Narrative Universe — Character Sheet

Player Name:

Pronouns:

Name:

Pronouns:

Class:

Ability Scores:

- Strength
- Dexterity
- Constitution
- Intelligence
- Wisdom
- Charisma

Level:

HP Total:

MP:

GP:

Offense Rating

Character Description:

Beliefs · Virtues · Flaws

Mana

Items & Equipment

Skills & Spells

Name	Action	Abilities	Notes

Appendix C: Sample Consent Form

Player		Narrator	

Campaign	
Theme/Tone	

Select the option that best describes how you feel about each topic below:
G = Green, consent for this topic to be included
Y = Yellow, Okay if topic remains veiled, discussion should be had before
R = Red, Hard no, do not include this topic

Creatures:

	G	Y	R
Bugs			
Rats			
Snakes			
Spiders			
Demons/Angels			
Other:			

Violence:

	G	Y	R
Blood			
Gore			
Graphic Descriptions			
Harm to Children			
Harm to Animals			

Relationships:

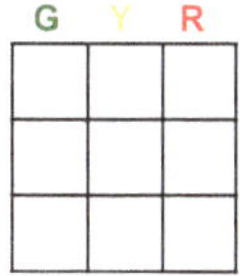

	G	Y	R
Inter-Party Conflict			
Inter-Party Fighting			
Inter-Party Romance			

Relationships (cont):

	G	Y	R
Party/NPC Romance			
Sex			

Mental/Emotional Health:

	G	Y	R
Claustrophobia			
Extreme Cold			
Extreme Heat			
Gaslighting			
Miscarriage/Abortion			
Natural Disasters			
Paralysis/Restraint			
Self Harm			
Sexual Assault			
Starvation			
Torture			
Thirst			

Real World Issues:

	G	Y	R
Homophobia			
Police Violence			
Racism			
Sexism			
Terrorism			
World Religions			

Other Topics:

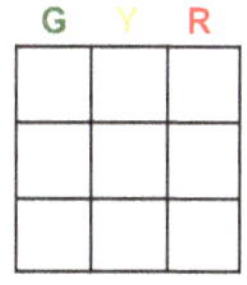

	G	Y	R

Appendix D: Worldbuilding

Designing a world of your own for your characters to explore can seem like a daunting task, but not all of the work needs to be done ahead of time by just the Narrator. Like anything else in the NU, worldbuilding should be a collaborative effort between all players at your table.

Some things you may want to consider when starting to build your world are:
- Major geographical features
- The people who inhabit this world
- Major historical events
- What function does magic play in this world?
- What function do the deities play in this world?
- What is currently going on around the world?
- What makes *this* world different from any other?

Starting Small

It isn't always necessary to begin worldbuild by looking at the entire scope of your setting. Sometimes it can be helpful to zoom way down into a single town, or even a single individual within that town.

- *Writing Prompt:* Imagine you are a person living in your new world. Write a short story about an ordinary day in the life of this person. Include as many details as you can, or as you like, regarding the other people you encounter and what you see and do during this day in your town.

Starting small gives you an opportunity to ground your new world in the daily lives of the people who live within it. You can begin generating a lot of ideas about how your

world functions at large by focusing on how it functions in a microcosm. After you have a solid picture of a single town or city, begin expanding outwards.

What are the nearby geographical features? Are there any other towns or cities nearby? How does your town interact with them? Does your town belong to a kingdom, or if not, what type of government does it have? Feel free to follow any rabbit holes you may discover while answering these questions as they can lead you towards discovering a great deal about your world.

Geography

Enchanted forests filled with magical lights, waterfalls cascading off of floating mountains shrouded in mist, vast underground caverns filled with unknown creatures… The geographical features of your new world can be a great tool to set the tone of your game before it even begins.

- *Writing Prompt:* Collect a handful of different dice as well as a large sheet of paper. Roll all of the dice at once onto the paper. Start by using any d20s rolled to create outlines of continents around your other dice. Assign features to other die shapes as you see fit - for example: d6s could be cities, d4s could be mountains, and d10s could be lakes and oceans. Now fill in the details of your world based on where the other dice landed on the paper.

As narrators of fictional worlds, we aren't bound by the same laws of physics dictating what is possible in our real world. Feel free to explore fantastical features that give your setting a unique feel.

- *Writing Prompt:* Come up with three distinct features of your world that do not exist in the real world, such as floating mountains, dragons or other creatures, and rivers made of pure magic. Now, write a short story about how these features came to be in your world, or their history within it. How do the unique features of your world affect the people who live within it?

People of the World

Worlds are not merely snapshots of a time the party may explore. They are as alive and ever changing as the people who live there. Giving details to the people and cultures that make up your world can help it feel vibrant and alive.

Elves, dwarves, orcs, dragons, and many many more peoples can inhabit your world, filling it with a diverse variety of peoples and cultures. Many fantasy settings are home to a variety of peoples, each with their own unique stories to tell.

It is important when creating histories and cultures for your world you do not rely on real world cultures or stereotypes. Not only could this be offensive to some players, but you also want to avoid misappropriating someone's culture for use in a game unless you properly understand it yourself.

Instead, fantasy games give us an opportunity to create worlds unaffected and unbound by many real world issues. While these games can be a powerful way to explore these real world issues in a safe environment, and give us an opportunity to grow our empathy, it is important all players at the table be on the same page about the type of game being played. If you wish to explore serious real-world issues, you should discuss this with the rest of the players during Session 0

History

Filling in historical details and events gives you as the Narrator a great basis for understanding where your world currently is. Providing these details as lore to your players can get them naturally invested in the mysteries of your new world and give them opportunities to explore more story hooks.

- *Writing Prompt:* Imagine how your world began. What are the three biggest events that have occurred since the beginning of your world that have shaped it into its current state? Using those three events as your major time periods, now think of three other important events that occurred between each period. You may continue to break down time periods this way as much as you wish until you have as many details about your world as you like.

Remember, worlds within the NU are places of magic, where powerful entities and gods may impose their influence, and multiple realms exist just beyond the mortal one.

Pantheon

The gods and deities of your world can play a much more active role in the lives of the people living there. With characters capable of not only channeling the powers of deities, but even of speaking with them, the influence of the divine is never too far off.

- *Writing Prompt:* Imagine a small town on an island. The people of this town are isolated from the rest of the world, and can only receive the supplies they need to survive from visitors to their island. What sort of supplies and assistance would the people of this island town hope for? What names or titles might they give those visitors?

While deities are often very powerful beings in your world, their influence is often rooted in fundamental aspects of their worshipers' lives. For instance, a deity of the sun might be prayed to by a community of farmers wanting a good yield for their crops, while a storm god might be worshiped by a coastal town in order to prevent disaster. Think about what the people of your world require in their daily lives and what ideals are important to them when creating your pantheon.

While you can draw inspiration for your pantheon from anywhere you like, you should discuss with your group during Session 0 how anyone feels about including deities from any real-world religions.

Group Prompts
The following prompts are designed to be done by your entire group to collaboratively build the world of your games together.

- Story Circle: One by one, go around your table with each player adding a new fact or piece of information to your world. You can always build upon what other players say, but can never remove a fact created by another player.
- The Webs We Weave: During character creation, have each player share their character's backstory with the rest of the group (in as much detail as they like). Then have each player choose one detail from another character's backstory to incorporate into their own. This encourages your characters to build a party that has connections with each other built into their backstories.
- Random Populations: Begin by rolling 2d10. Then each player goes around the table adding a different society, people, or nation to the world. Continue until you have as many populations as the number you rolled. Players may choose to add fantasy peoples to the world, or make up their own.
- Name Game: Either before beginning your campaign, or an individual session, ask the other players at the table to come up with a list of names. These can be names for people or locations in your world. Use these names to inspire NPCs and locations within your world the party can visit. Encourage players to add some detail to their names. For example: Bob the kindly carrot farmer rather than simply…Bob.
- The Game Before the Game: This method works best if your group enjoys playing a board game with a map that players place pieces onto during play. Pick a board game of your group's choice and play a game of it before beginning your campaign. At the end of the game, take note of the final position of the player's pieces, and any details about the game you wish to include. Use this to inspire your world, especially political alliances and the positions of rivaling kingdoms.

Appendix E: Class Skill Lists

- Special* (Sp*) - See skill description on listed page for details

Bard

Skill Name	Action Type	Reliant Abilities	Req.	Page #
Able Learner	Prep	All		60
Acrobatics	Utility	Dex		60
Allegro	Def	Cha		61
Appraise	Exp	Int, Wis		61
Archaeology	Exp	Int, Wis		61
Bardic Knowledge	Exp	Int, Wis		63
Battle Caster	Feature	All	5	64
Breadth of Experience	Feature	All		65
Cannot be Deleted	Feature	Con, Wis	7	66
Cannot be Disintegrated	Feature	Con	10	66
Cannot be Unmade	Feature	Con, Cha	15	66
Can't Hit That Face	Def	Cha		66
Certainty	Feature	Wis	5	66
Charismatic Liar	Utility	Cha		67
Climbing	Exp	Str, Con		67
Cooperative	Utility	Wis		69
Countersong	Def	Int, Cha		69
Crafting	Prep	Special*		70
Create Opportunity	Def, Utility	Wis		70
Deathless	Feature	All	10	71
Deception	Utility	Cha		72
Decipher Script	Prep	Int		72
Defensive Casting	Def	Int, Wis		72
Diplomacy	Utility	Cha		73
Dungeoneering	Exp	Int, Wis		76

Enhanced Perception	Feature	Wis		77
Enhance Personal Narrative	Utility	Wis, Cha		77
Extra Mana	Feature	All		78
Fae Ecology	Exp	Int		78
Fae Protocols	Social	Cha		78
False Reputation	Feature	Cha		78
Fascinate	Def, Utility	Cha		79
Financial Backers	Feature	Cha	Sp*	80
Foraging	Exp	Int, Wis		80
Forging	Prep	Str, Int		80
Gather Information	Exp	Int, Cha		81
Haggling	Social	Cha		82
Harmful Roast	Off	Cha		82
Hey, I Like Their Vibe	Social	Cha		82
Historical Knowledge	Exp	Int		83
Identify Device	Exp	Int		83
Improved Ability	Feature	Special*	5	83
Improved Skill Critical	Feature	Special*	5	84
Innocent Appearance	Social	Cha		85
Insight	Social	Wis		85
Inspire Courage	Def	Wis, Cha		85
Intimidation	Social	Cha		85
Investigation	Exp	Int		85
Iron Will	Feature	Wis		85
Jack of All Trades (10%)	Utility	Special*		86
Keen Ear	Utility	Int		86
Legendary Defenses	Utility	All	20	86
Legerdemain	Utility	Dex		86
Local Connections	Prep	Cha		87

Local Knowledge	Exp	Int		87
Monster Ecology	Exp	Int		90
Mortal Protocols	Social	Int		90
Musical Talent	Special*	Wis		13
Organize Alliance	Social	Cha		92
Perception	Utility	Int		93
Perfect Time Keeping	Feature	Int		93
Persuasion	Utility	Cha		93
Performance	Prep	Cha		94
Planar Ecology	Exp	Int		94
Planar Protocols	Social	Int		94
Plan B	Prep	Int		95
Royal Protocols	Social	Int		96
Sleight of Hand	Utility	Dex		98
Slippery Mind	Feature	Wis		99
Skillful	Feature	All		99
Storytelling	Social	Cha		100
Swimming	Exp	Str, Con		101
Thieves Guild Membership	Feature	Cha		101
Time Slip	Feature	All	10	101
Trust Me, I Know a Guy	Prep	Cha		102
Unnoticeable	Exp	Dex, Wis		102
Upper Realm Protocols	Social	Cha		103
Walk in Like I Own the Place	Utility	Cha		103
Woodland Ecology	Exp	Int		103

Charlatan

Skill Name	Action Type	Reliant Abilities	Req.	Page #
Able Learner	Prep	All		60
Alms for the Poor	Prep	Cha		61
Attract Attention	Social, Def	Cha		62
Aura of Belief	Utility	Cha		62
Aura of Temptation	Social	Cha		62
Battle Caster	Feature	All	5	64
Cannot be Deleted	Feature	Con, Wis	7	66
Cannot be Disintegrated	Feature	Con	10	66
Cannot be Unmade	Feature	Con, Cha	15	66
Can't Hit That Face	Def	Cha		66
Cause Fear	Off	Cha		66
Certainty	Feature	Wis	5	66
Charismatic Liar	Social	Cha		67
Climbing	Exp	Str, Con		67
Commune with Random Deity	Prep	Cha		68
Concentration	Prep, Def	Wis		68
Confusing Revelations	Prep	Wis		69
Cooperative	Utility	Wis		69
Crafting	Prep	Special*		70
Create Opportunity	Def, Utility	Wis		70
Cult Leader	Feature	Cha	10	70
Death Bless	Feature	All	5	71
Death Curse	Feature	All	5	71
Deathless	Feature	All	10	71
Deception	Utility	Cha		72
Defensive Casting	Def	Int, Wis		72

Desperate Prayer	Feature	Cha	15	73
Devil in your Ear	Feature	Wis		73
Diplomacy	Utility	Cha		73
Disciple of Pain	Feature	Wis		74
Divine Interdiction	Def	Wis		74
Enhanced Perception	Feature	Wis		77
False Reputation	Feature	Cha		78
Financial Backers	Feature	Cha	Sp*	80
Flexible Prayer	Utility	Int, Wis	12	80
Foraging	Exp	Int, Wis		80
Forging	Prep	Str, Int		80
Gather Congregation	Prep	Wis, Cha		81
Gather Information	Exp	Int, Cha		81
Harmful Roast	Off	Cha		82
Hey, I Like Their Vibe	Social	Cha		82
Hidden Faith	Prep	Wis		83
Historical Knowledge	Exp	Int		83
Improved Ability	Feature	Special*	5	83
Improved Skill Critical	Feature	Special*	5	84
Innocent Appearance	Social	Cha		85
Insight	Social	Wis		85
Intimidation	Social	Cha		85
Investigation	Exp	Int		85
Iron Will	Feature	Wis		85
Lay on Hands	Def	Wis		86
Legendary Defenses	Utility	All	20	86
Lower Realm Connections	Prep	Cha	6	87
Lower Realm Protocols	Utility	Cha		88
Member of the Congregation	Feature	Cha		89

Misguided Hand	Prep	Cha		90
Mortal Protocols	Social	Int		90
Nonsensical Divine Countenance	Prep, Def	Cha		91
Oracle	Feature	Wis		92
Pathetic Plea	Def	Cha		93
Perception	Utility	Int		93
Perfect Time Keeping	Feature	Int		93
Persuasion	Utility	Cha		93
Plan B	Prep	Int		95
Religious Knowledge	Exp	Int		95
Royal Protocols	Social	Int		96
Self-Righteous Flame	Off	Cha, OR		97
Servant of Any Deity	Prep	Cha	5	97
Silent Prayer	Feature	Wis	6	98
Simony	Feature	Wis		98
Slippery Mind	Feature	Wis		99
Skillful	Feature	All		99
Swimming	Exp	Str, Con		101
Tearful Confession	Def	Cha		101
Time Slip	Feature	All	10	101
Upper Realm Connection	Prep	Cha	6	103
Upper Realm Travel	Prep	Cha	11	103
Upper Realm Protocols	Social	Cha		103

Druid

Skill Name	Action Type	Reliant Abilities	Req.	Page #
Able Learner	Prep	All		60
Animal Languages	Exp	Int, Cha		61
Aura of Nature	Prep, Def	Wis		63
Battle Caster	Feature	All	5	64
Beastial Aspect	Utility	Con, Wis		64
Bolstered Resilience	Utility	Con, Wis		64
Breadth of Experience	Feature	All		65
Cannot be Deleted	Feature	Con, Wis	7	66
Cannot be Disintegrated	Feature	Con	10	66
Cannot be Unmade	Feature	Con, Cha	15	66
Can't Hit That Face	Def	Cha		66
Certainty	Feature	Wis	5	66
Channel Nature's Power	Off	Con, Wis		66
Charge of the Herd Beast	Off	Str		67
Circle Initiate	Feature	Wis, Cha		67
Climbing	Exp	Str, Con		67
Commune with Deity	Preparation	Wis, Cha		68
Commune with Nature	Exploration	Wis, Cha		68
Concentration	Prep, Def	Wis		68
Cooperative	Utility	Wis		69
Crafting	Prep	Special*		70
Create Opportunity	Def, Utility	Wis		70
Death Bless	Feature	All	5	71
Death Curse	Feature	All	5	71
Deathless	Feature	All	10	71
Deception	Utility	Cha		72
Defile	Off	Wis		72

Defensive Casting	Def	Int, Wis		72
Divine Interdiction	Def	Wis		74
Druidic Companion	Prep	Wis, Cha	2	75
Druidic Familiar	Prep	Wis	5	75
Druidic Rituals	Prep	All	7	75
Efficacious Healer	Feature	Wis		76
Eminence	Prep	Wis		76
Enhanced Perception	Feature	Wis		77
Fae Connection	Prep	Cha		78
Fae Ecology	Exp	Int		78
Fae Protocols	Social	Cha		78
Financial Backers	Feature	Cha	Sp*	80
Foraging	Exploration	Int, Wis		80
Forging	Prep	Str, Int		80
Gather Animal Congress	Def	Wis, Cha	10	81
Gather Information	Exp	Int, Cha		81
Hidden Faith	Prep	Wis		83
Holy Oath	Feature	Special*	Sp*	83
Improved Ability	Feature	Special*	5	83
Improved Skill Critical	Feature	Special*	5	84
Insight	Social	Wis		85
Intimidation	Social	Cha		85
Investigation	Exp	Int		85
Iron Will	Feature	Wis		85
Lay on Hands	Def	Wis		86
Legendary Defenses	Utility	All		86
Medicinal Herbs	Exp	Int, Wis		89
Meditation	Prep	Wis		89
Monster Ecology	Exp	Int		90

Mortal Protocols	Social	Int		90
Natural Life	Def	Wis	15	90
Nature's Bard	Feature	Cha		91
Nature's Bloom	Feature	All	20	91
Nature's Guidance	Prep, Def	Wis		91
Perception	Utility	Int		93
Perfect Time Keeping	Feature	Int		93
Persuasion	Utility	Cha		93
Plan B	Prep	Int		95
Sense Faith	Social	Wis		97
Servant of Nature	Feature	Wis	5	97
Shadow of the Great Tree	Exp	Wis	10	98
Silent Prayer	Feature	Wis	6	98
Slippery Mind	Feature	Wis		99
Skillful	Feature	All		99
Swimming	Exp	Str, Con		101
Time Slip	Feature	All	10	101
Unnoticeable	Exp	Dex, Wis		102
Upper Planar Protocols	Social	Cha		103
Woodland Ecology	Exp	Int		103

Fighter

Skill Name	Action Type	Reliant Abilities	Req.	Page #
Able Learner	Prep	All		60
Acrobatics	Utility	Dex		60
Ambush	Special*	Dex, Wis		61
Armored Skin	Feature	Con	5	62
Armored Fighting	Feature	Con		62
Battle Ready	Feature	Wis		64
Braced Strike	Off	OR		65
Break Action Sequence	Def	Wis		65
Called Shot	Feature	Dex, Int		65
Cannot be Deleted	Feature	Con, Wis	7	66
Cannot be Disintegrated	Feature	Con	10	66
Cannot be Unmade	Feature	Con, Cha	15	66
Certainty	Feature	Wis	5	66
Climbing	Exp	Str, Con		67
Combat Expertise	Utility	Int		67
Combat Readiness	Feature	Dex		67
Commander	Utility	Cha		67
Cooperative	Utility	Wis		69
Crack in the Defenses	Utility	Int		70
Crafting	Prep	Special*		70
Create Opportunity	Def, Utility	Wis		70
Damage Reduction	Feature	Con	10	71
Deathless	Feature	All	10	71
Deception	Utility	Cha		72
Deflection	Def	Dex		72
Devastating Critical	Feature	Str, OR		73
Dire Charge	Off	Str		74

Disarm	Off	OR		74
Distant Shot	Feature	Dex		74
Dodge	Def	Dex		75
Dual Wielding	Feature	Str, Dex		75
Energy Resistance	Feature	Con		77
Endurance	Utility	Con		77
Enhanced Perception	Feature	Wis		77
Favored Weapon	Feature	Wis	6	79
Feint	Utility	Int, Cha		79
Fight Dirty	Off	Dex, Wis		79
Fighting Blind	Feature	Wis	5	79
Financial Backers	Feature	Cha	Sp*	80
Foraging	Exp	Int, Wis		80
Forging	Prep	Str, Int		80
Gather Information	Exp	Int, Cha		81
Hearty	Feature	Con		82
Heavy Weapon Fighting	Feature	Str		82
Improved Ability	Feature	Special*	5	83
Improved Critical Strike	Feature	OR	5	84
Improved Skill Critical	Feature	Special*	5	84
Insight	Social	Wis		85
Intimidation	Social	Cha		85
Investigation	Exp	Int		85
Iron Will	Feature	Wis		85
Leadership	Utility	Wis		86
Legendary Defenses	Utility	All	20	86
Lightning Reflexes	Utility	Dex	Sp*	87
Magic Resistance (10%)	Feature	Special*	6	88
Manyshot	Off	Dex		88

Mobility	Utility	Dex	5	90
Monster Ecology	Exp	Int		90
Mortal Protocols	Social	Int		90
Mounted Combatant	Feature	Cha		90
No Quick Deaths	Feature	Con		92
Organize Alliance	Social	Cha		92
Overwhelming Critical	Feature	OR		92
Parry	Def	Str, Dex		92
Penetrate Armor	Feature	OR		93
Perception	Utility	Int		93
Perfect Time Keeping	Feature	Int		93
Persuasion	Utility	Cha		93
Plan B	Prep	Int		95
Prowess	Utility	Int		95
Rending Attack	Utility	Str		96
Shield Bash	Feature	OR		98
Shot on the Run	Utility	Dex, Wis		98
Slippery Mind	Feature	Wis		99
Skillful	Feature	All		99
Spellcasting Harrier	Def	Cha		99
Spring Attack	Off	Dex, OR		99
Storm of Throws	Off	Str, OR	Sp*	100
Stunning Blow	Off	OR		100
Swarm of Arrows	Off	Dex, OR	Sp*	100
Swimming	Exp	Str, Con		101
Time Slip	Feature	All	10	101
Trip Attack	Off	Dex, OR		102
Upper Realm Protocols	Social	Cha		103
Whirlwind Attack	Off	OR		103

Woodland Ecology	Exp	Int		103
Wrestler	Off	Str, Dex		104

Mage

Skill Name	Action Type	Reliant Abilities	Req.	Page #
Able Learner	Prep	All		60
Alchemy	Prep	Int, Wis		60
Appraise	Exp	Int, Wis		61
Archaeology	Exp	Int, Wis		61
Battle Caster	Feature	All	5	64
Cannot be Deleted	Feature	Con, Wis	7	66
Cannot be Disintegrated	Feature	Con	10	66
Cannot be Unmade	Feature	Con, Cha	15	66
Certainty	Feature	Wis	5	66
Climbing	Exp	Str, Con		67
Concentration	Prep, Def	Wis		68
Contingency Plan	Prep	Int, Wis	7	69
Cooperative	Utility	Wis		69
Crafting	Prep	Special*		70
Create Opportunity	Def, Utility	Wis		70
Deathless	Feature	All	10	71
Deception	Utility	Cha		72
Decipher Script	Prep	Int		72
Defensive Casting	Def	Int, Wis		72
Elemantalist	Feature	Int, Wis	4	76
Enchanting	Prep	Int, Wis	5	76
Enhanced Perception	Feature	Wis		77
Extra Mana	Feature	All		78

Skill Name	Action Type	Reliant Abilities	Req.	Page #
Able Learner	Prep	All		60
Alchemy	Prep	Int, Wis		60
Appraise	Exp	Int, Wis		61
Archaeology	Exp	Int, Wis		61
Battle Caster	Feature	All	5	64
Cannot be Deleted	Feature	Con, Wis	7	66
Cannot be Disintegrated	Feature	Con	10	66
Cannot be Unmade	Feature	Con, Cha	15	66
Certainty	Feature	Wis	5	66
Climbing	Exp	Str, Con		67
Fae Connection	Prep	Cha		78
Fae Ecology	Exp	Int		78
Fae Protocols	Social	Cha		78
Financial Backers	Feature	Cha	Sp*	80
Focus	Prep	Wis		80
Foraging	Exp	Int, Wis		80
Forging	Prep	Str, Int		80
Gather Elements	Prep	Int, Wis		81
Gather Information	Exp	Int, Cha		81
Historical Knowledge	Exp	Int		83
Identify Device	Exp	Int		83
Improved Ability	Feature	Special*	5	83
Improved Skill Critical	Feature	Special*	5	84
Improved Summoning	Feature	Cha		84
Insight	Social	Wis		85
Intimidation	Social	Cha		85
Investigation	Exp	Int		85
Iron Will	Feature	Wis		85

Skill Name	Action Type	Reliant Abilities	Req.	Page #
Able Learner	Prep	All		60
Alchemy	Prep	Int, Wis		60
Appraise	Exp	Int, Wis		61
Archaeology	Exp	Int, Wis		61
Battle Caster	Feature	All	5	64
Cannot be Deleted	Feature	Con, Wis	7	66
Cannot be Disintegrated	Feature	Con	10	66
Cannot be Unmade	Feature	Con, Cha	15	66
Certainty	Feature	Wis	5	66
Climbing	Exp	Str, Con		67
Legendary Defenses	Utility	All	20	86
Lower Realm Connections	Prep	Cha	6	87
Lower Realm Protocols	Social	Cha		88
Mage's Disruption	Def	Int, Wis		88
Mage Guild Membership	Feature	Int		88
Meditation	Prep	Wis		89
Monster Ecology	Exp	Int		90
Mortal Protocols	Social	Int		90
Perception	Utility	Int		93
Perfect Time Keeping	Feature	Int		93
Persuasion	Utility	Cha		93
Performance	Prep	Cha		94
Planar Ecology	Exp	Int		94
Planar Patron	Prep	Cha	8	94
Planar Protocols	Social	Int		94
Plan B	Prep	Int		95
Quickened Casting	Feature	Int	12	95
Reduce Mana Cost	Feature	Int, Wis	8	95

Skill Name	Action Type	Reliant Abilities	Req.	Page #
Able Learner	Prep	All		60
Alchemy	Prep	Int, Wis		60
Appraise	Exp	Int, Wis		61
Archaeology	Exp	Int, Wis		61
Battle Caster	Feature	All	5	64
Cannot be Deleted	Feature	Con, Wis	7	66
Cannot be Disintegrated	Feature	Con	10	66
Cannot be Unmade	Feature	Con, Cha	15	66
Certainty	Feature	Wis	5	66
Climbing	Exp	Str, Con		67
Research	Prep	Int		15
Royal Protocols	Social	Int		96
Sculpt Spell	Feature	Int	7	96
Sleight of Hand	Utility	Dex		98
Slippery Mind	Feature	Wis		99
Skillful	Feature	All		99
Spellcrafting	Prep	Int, Wis	5	99
Swimming	Exp	Str, Con		101
Thaumaturgy	Prep	Int, Wis		101
Time Slip	Feature	All	10	101
Upper Realm Connection	Prep	Cha	6	103
Upper Realm Protocols	Social	Cha		103

Priest

Skill Name	Action Type	Reliant Abilities	Req.	Page #
Able Learner	Prep	All		60
Abundant Revelations	Prep	Wis		60
Aura of Conviction	Off	Wis		62
Aura of the Divine	Def	Wis		63
Battle Caster	Feature	All	5	64
Bolstered Resilience	Utility	Con, Wis		64
Boundless Optimism	Feature	Cha		64
Branded for Retribution	Utility	Wis		65
Breadth of Experience	Feature	All		65
Cannot be Deleted	Feature	Con, Wis	7	66
Cannot be Disintegrated	Feature	Con	10	66
Cannot be Unmade	Feature	Con, Cha	15	66
Can't Hit That Face	Def	Charisma		66
Certainty	Feature	Wis	5	66
Climbing	Exp	Str, Con		67
Commune with Deity	Prep	Wis, Cha		68
Concentration	Prep, Def	Wis		68
Confession	Def	Wis, Cha		68
Conviction	Feature	Wis	15	69
Cooperative	Utility	Wis		69
Crafting	Prep	Special*		70
Create Opportunity	Def, Utility	Wis		70
Cult Leader	Feature	Cha	10	70
Death Bless	Feature	All	5	71
Death Curse	Feature	All	5	71

Deathless	Feature	All	10	71
Deception	Utility	Cha		72
Decipher Script	Prep	Int		72
Defensive Casting	Def	Int, Wis		72
Demon Hunter	Feature	Wis, Cha	5	72
Diplomacy	Utility	Cha		73
Disciple of Pain	Feature	Wis		74
Divine Bard	Feature	Cha	10	74
Divine Interdiction	Defensive	Wis		74
Efficacious Healer	Feature	Wis		76
Enhanced Perception	Feature	Wis		77
Exorcist	Feature	Wis		77
Faithful Servant	Prep	Wis		78
Financial Backers	Feature	Cha	Sp*	80
Flexible Prayer	Utility	Int, Wis	12	80
Foraging	Exp	Int, Wis		80
Forging	Prep	Str, Int		80
Gather Congregation	Prep	Wis, Cha		81
Gather Information	Exp	Int, Cha		81
Guided Hand	Utility	Wis		81
Hey, I Like Their Vibe	Social	Cha		82
Hidden Faith	Prep	Wis		83
Historical Knowledge	Exp	Int		83
Holy Writ	Feature	Wis, Cha		16
Holy Oath	Feature	Special*	Sp*	83
Holy Rebuke	Off	Wis		83
Improved Ability	Feature	Special*	5	83
Improved Skill Critical	Feature	Special*	5	84
In the Shadow of your Wings	Def	Wis	10	84

Insight	Social	Wis		85
Intimidation	Social	Cha		85
Investigation	Exp	Int		85
Iron Will	Feature	Wis		85
Lay on Hands	Def	Wis		86
Legendary Defenses	Utility	All	20	86
Lesser Demesne	Prep, Special*	Wis	15	87
Lower Realm Connections	Prep	Cha	6	87
Lower Realm Protocols	Social	Cha		88
Martyrdom	Off	All	12	89
Medicine	Utility	Int, Wis		89
Meditation	Prep	Wis		89
Mortal Protocols	Social	Int		90
Oracle	Feature	Wis		92
Perception	Utility	Int		93
Perfect Time Keeping	Feature	Int		93
Persuasion	Utility	Cha		93
Planar Ecology	Exp	Int		94
Plan B	Prep	Int		95
Religious Knowledge	Exp	Int		95
Resist Fear	Def	Wis		96
Righteous Flame	Off	Wis, OR		96
Royal Protocols	Social	Int		96
Sense Faith	Social	Wis		97
Silent Prayer	Feature	Wis	6	98
Slippery Mind	Feature	Wis		99
Skillful	Feature	All		99
Swimming	Exp	Str, Con		101
Temple Sigil	Feature	Wis, Cha		101

Time Slip	Feature	All	10	101
Undying Faith	Feature	Wis	15	102
Unholy Rebuke	Off	Cha		102
Upper Realm Connection	Prep	Cha	6	103
Upper Realm Travel	Prep	Cha	11	103
Upper Realm Protocols	Social	Cha		103

Rogue

Skill Name	Action Type	Reliant Abilities	Req.	Page #
Able Learner	Prep	All		60
Acrobatics	Utility	Dex		60
Ambush	Special*	Dex, Wis		61
Archaeology	Exp	Int, Wis		61
Backstab (10%)	Off	Special		63
Battle Ready	Feature	Wis		64
Break Action Sequence	Def	Wis		65
Cannot be Deleted	Feature	Con, Wis	7	66
Cannot be Disintegrated	Feature	Con	10	66
Cannot be Unmade	Feature	Con, Cha	15	66
Certainty	Feature	Wis	5	66
Charismatic Liar	Utility	Cha		67
Climbing	Exp	Str, Con		67
Combat Readiness	Feature	Dex		67
Cooperative	Utility	Wis		69
Crack in the Defenses	Utility	Int		70
Crafting	Prep	Special*		70
Create Opportunity	Def, Utility	Wis		70
Deathless	Feature	All	10	71

Deception	Utility	Cha		72
Decipher Script	Prep	Int		72
Detect Trap (10%)	Exp	Special		73
Detect Treasure (10%)	Exp	Special		73
Diplomacy	Utility	Cha		73
Dodge	Def	Dex		75
Dungeoneering	Exp	Int, Wis		76
Enhanced Perception	Feature	Wis		77
Evasion (10%)	Def	Special*		77
Fae Ecology	Exp	Int		78
Fae Protocols	Social	Cha		78
Fight Dirty	Off	Dex, Wis		79
Financial Backers	Feature	Cha	Sp*	80
Foraging	Exp	Int, Wis		80
Forging	Prep	Str, Int		80
Gather Information	Exp	Int, Cha		81
Haggling	Social	Cha		82
Hey, I Like Their Vibe	Social	Cha		82
Historical Knowledge	Exp	Int		83
Identify Device	Exp	Int		83
Improved Ability	Feature	Special*	5	83
Improved Skill Critical	Feature	Special*	5	84
Incredible Luck (5%)	Utility	Special*		84
Innocent Appearance	Social	Cha		85
Insight	Social	Wis		85
Intimidation	Social	Cha		85
Investigation	Exp	Int		85
Iron Will	Feature	Wis		85
Jack of All Trades (10%)	Utility	Special*		86

Legendary Defenses	Utility	All	20	86
Lightning Reflexes	Utility	Dex	Sp*	87
Local Connections	Prep	Cha		87
Local Knowledge	Exp	Int		87
Mobility	Utility	Dex	5	90
Monster Ecology	Exp	Int		90
Mortal Protocols	Social	Int		90
Open Lock (10%)	Exp	Special*		92
Parry	Def	Str, Dex		92
Perception	Utility	Int		93
Perfect Response (10%)	Utility	Special*		93
Perfect Time Keeping	Feature	Int		93
Persuasion	Utility	Cha		93
Pickpocket (10%)	Utility	Special*		94
Plan B	Prep	Int		95
Read Magic Scroll	Utility	Int		95
Royal Protocols	Social	Int		96
Sleight of Hand	Utility	Dex		98
Slippery Mind	Feature	Wis		99
Skillful	Feature	All		99
Stealth (10%)	Exp	Special*		100
Swimming	Exp	Str, Con		101
Thieves Guild Membership	Feature	Cha		101
Time Slip	Feature	All	10	101
Trip Attack	Off	Dex, OR		102
Trust Me, I Know a Guy	Prep	Cha		102
Underworld Connections	Prep	Cha		102
Unnoticeable	Exp	Dex, Wis		102
Upper Realm Protocols	Social	Cha		103

Walk in Like I Own the Place	Utility	Cha		103
Woodland Ecology	Exp	Int		103

Chapter 16: Glossaries

Glossary of Tables

	discretion

Charlatan Prayer Failure Chance - pg 13

Charlatan Level	Spell Failure Range
1-3	40 and below
4-7	33 and below
8-10	25 and below
11-14	15 and below
15-19	10 and below
20+	5 and below

Druid Transformation - pg 14

Animal form	Spell Level
Small creature	1
Medium creature	3
Large creature	5
Creature with special movement (flying, swimming, burrowing)	4
Magical creatures	*Narrator's

Cost per Equipment Level - pg 18

Equipment Level:	Recommended Cost:
Basic	0-1,000 mp
Specialized	1,000-5,000 mp
Artisan	5,000 - 25,000 mp
Wondrous	25,000 - 100,000 mp
Unique	100,000+ mp

Magical Item Enchantments - pg 22

Effect	Points
Access to a skill	+1 / level of skill
Access to a spell/prayer, 1/day	+1 / each spell level
Additional uses of a spell/prayer per day	+1 / spell level for each additional usage
Single-use (potion or scroll)	-2 points

Equipment Level	Total Points
Artisan	1-3

Wondrous	4-6
Unique	7-10

81-95	Breaking
95-100	Devastating

NPC Attitudes - pg 27

Percentage (1-100)	Attitude
1-10	Hated enemy
11-25	Bitter rival, sever mistrust
25-33	Dislike, untrusting, suspicious
34-45	Cautious, wary
45-65	Polite, cordial, acquaintances
65-75	Friendly, familiar
76-89	Trusted friends, allies
90-100	Like family

Storytelling Damage Table - pg 31

Fate Roll result	Damage level
1-10	Glancing
11-25	Superficial
26-40	Cutting
41-60	Injuring
61-80	Wounding

Base Fate Roll Table - pg 37

Result	Impact
1	Catastrophic impact on the party and game
2-10	"Worst case scenario" outcomes
11-25	Very bad outcome, little to no positive
26-40	Poor outcome, presents a difficult path ahead
41-59	Mixed outcome, party may get what they want but at a cost
60-74	Positive outcome for the party but with some setback or difficulty
75-89	Very good outcome for the party, nearly all positive
90-99	"Best case scenario" outcomes
100	Deus-ex-machina like outcome for the party

Favorable Fate Roll Table - pg 39

Result	Impact
1 - 10	Very bad outcome, little to no positive
11 - 33	Poor outcome, but potentially redeemable
34 - 50	Mixed outcome, party may get what they want but at a cost
51 - 66	Positive outcome for the party but with some minor setback or difficulty
66 - 84	Very good outcome for the party, nearly all positive
85 - 99	"Best case scenario" outcomes
100	Deus-ex-machina like outcome for the party

Unfavorable Fate Roll Table - pg 40

Result	Impact

100 - 91	Very good outcome for the party, nearly all positive
90 - 75	Mostly positive outcome with some cost or drawback
74 - 60	Mixed success, party may get what they want but at a cost
59 - 40	Poor outcome, presents a difficult path ahead
39 - 20	Very bad outcome, a clear danger or threat to the party
19 - 2	"Worse case scenario" outcomes
1	Catastrophic, campaign altering outcome

Random Character Interactions - pg 44

Result	Situation
1	One of the characters needs help from the other
2	The two characters get into a disagreement
3	One of the characters confides something with the other
4	The two characters discover something new in camp
5	The two characters get lost during the preparation round

6	One of the characters tells the other a secret
7	The two characters notice something new about another party member
8	One of the characters tells the other a rumor they've heard
9	The two characters find themselves alone together
10	One of the characters confesses something to the other

Variable Cost Spell Table - Pg 106

Mana Used	Spell Effects
1	Trivial effect on a single person
5	Moderate effect on a single person
9	Significant effect on a single person
20	Moderate effect on a small group
30	Significant effect on a small group
40	Moderate effect on a general area or fantastic effect on a single person
50	Significant effect on a general area
75	Minor reality shaping effects
100+	Near mastery over Spell's effects

- Offensive - Combat round skills used to attack your enemies
- Defensive - Combat round skills used to defend yourself or your allies

Attitude: A measure of how helpful or unfriendly an NPC is, can be improved (or possibly worsened) by Social Skills.

Boon: Gift of divine favor from a powerful being, allowing you to determine the outcome of a Fate Roll. Boons are an optional rule.

Bonus: Any positive modifier given to a character's roll through the use of skills or from the Narrator.

Campaign: A long-form game played out over a number of Sessions to tell a complex narrative and follow the same Characters from beginning to end.

Class: Describes a character's primary skillset. Each Class in the NU has a Core Ability, granting a unique feature to that class, as well as a list of Skills available for characters of that class to train. Classes presented in this book are:
- Bard
- Charlatan
- Druid
- Fighter
- Mage
- Priest
- Rogue

Character: Fictional individuals created by the players to interact with the story the Narrator tells.

Core Ability: The unique ability or feature granted by each Class at Level 1.

Glossary of Terms

Ability: Description of your character's physical and mental traits including:
- Strength
- Dexterity
- Constitution
- Intelligence
- Wisdom
- Charisma

Ability Score: Numerical value assigned to each ability used in determining the success of Skill Checks

Action: Any way of your characters interacting with and changing the story, normally through the use of Skills and Spells.

Action Type: Detail listed in a Skill's description defining what round it may be most useful to use during. Action types include:
- Preparation - Skills that help your character prepare for a day of adventure
- Exploration - Skills that help you gain information about your environment or safely traverse through it
- Social - Skills that help you improve the Attitude of NPCs
- Enduring Feature - A passive bonus your character gains
- Utility - Flexible skills usable in a number of situations

Crafting: The ability for characters to create new pieces of equipment using Gathering Points.

Current Percentage: The success rate of Rogue's Percentage Skills. Initial Current Percentage is listed after each Skill in **Chapter 11.**

Encounters: Situations or conflicts the party must use their skills and spells in order to solve. The three primary types of encounters are:
- Exploration - Encounters dealing with environmental dangers
- Combat - Encounters where the characters are physically fighting an enemy
- Social - A special type of Encounter that may occur during any Round.

Equipment: The tools and gear your character has at their disposal. Equipment may include:
- Toolkits - Used in Crafting or to give a specific skill a Bonus.
- Armor - Protective equipment for your Character, available in light, medium, heavy, and shields.
- Weapons - Any tool designed to harm an opponent. Weapons primarily serve an aesthetic purpose in game.
- Magic Items - Any piece of equipment permanently enchanted with a Spell.

Fate Roll: Made to determine how good or bad the narrative outcome of a character's actions are. Made with a 100 sided die.

Gathering Points: Generic term in the NU used to describe raw materials that your character may use to craft new pieces of equipment.

Health Points: A measure of your character's stamina and ability to continue fighting. When reduced to 0, your character falls unconscious.

Level: Used to keep track of your character's progress within a Class as well as their overall power. Levels are granted by the Narrator when the party reaches significant points in the story.

Money Points: Generic term in the NU used to describe the total sum of cash, gold, and easily sold valuable items.

Narrator: The player at the table given responsibility for interpreting Fate Rolls, determining mechanics, and narrating the action of the game.

NPC: Short for Non-Player Character, these are any character that is controlled by the Narrator.

Penalty: Any negative modifier given to a character's roll through the use of skills or from the Narrator.

Percentage Skills: Unique Skills gained by Rogues that rely on a percentage success rather than on a reliant ability.

Player: The real life humans who have come together to tell a story through this game.

Reliant Ability: Detail listed in a Skill's description listing which abilities are used to determine the outcome of a Skill Check.

Roll-Under System: The system used to determine if a Skill Check succeeds or fails. You must *roll* a number *under* your

Character's ability score to achieve a success.

Round: A segment of time in the game during which each Character gets to take an action. The three primary types of rounds are:

- Preparation - A time for characters to train skills, craft items, and gather information. Typically represents 3-4 hours of time.
- Exploration - Traversing dangerous environments, either wilderness or dungeon-like. Typically represents 30 minutes to an hour of time.
- Combat - Combat rounds usually describe a brief period where each combatant may take an Offensive or Defensive action.

Rule Zero: Skills are the narrative, the Narrator is the mechanics.

Session: A single "game" of the Narrative Universe. Sessions are typically a few hours long but can be as long or short as your group wishes. If your Campaign is a television show, each Session is a single episode.

Session 0: Initial meeting of players before the official start of a campaign to discuss aspects of the story and characters.

Skill: Talents and abilities possessed by your character. One of the two primary types of Actions in the NU.

Skill Check: Used to determine if a character is successful or not when using one of their Skills. Made with a 20 sided die.

Spell: Magical abilities granted to some classes that don't require a Skill Check.

- **Prayer:** Spells granted to certain classes directly from a deity or higher power.

TTRPG: Short for Tabletop Roleplaying Game, a game where players meet to tell a story together using their imaginations, dice, and pencil & paper.

Worldbuilding: The process of creating your own world or setting for players to explore in games.

Chapter 16: Acknowledgments

Joshua Orsak is the creator of the NU TTYPG system. He is a 44 year-old professional TTRPG game runner from Houston, Texas where he lives with his wife Angelic. He has been running the NU system that he and his friends invented for 28 years and has been running games professionally for a decade. He runs the Orsak Narrative Universe pro gaming Discord where he spends most of his time. He is also a competitive dancer and competes around the country with this world-class coach Olga.

Joshua would like to thank his brother, Jeremiah Orsak. Samuel Chiapetta and his brother Nick who helped develop the NU system 28 years ago. Wyatt Griffis, Sean Reynolds, and CJ Tolman who helped it grow. Kara Kurzeja who helped organize it for publication and fund it. His wife Angelic Covarrubia who makes everything happen. And his dance coach Olga Richardson who inspired me to do things I never thought possible.

Daisy Stridinger is the writer of this book and helped adapt the NU system for publication. He is a writer, actor, director, and content creator from Pittsburgh, Pennsylvania. Kurt has been a professional content creator for 2 years and can be found online under the name MrKurtwise. In addition to his content work, Kurt also directs and performs with an educational theater in Pittsburgh, and enjoys spending his time playing board games and painting with his fiance.

Kurt would like to thank Joshua Orsak and the entire Orsak Narrative Universe for welcoming him into their community and putting their trust in him for this project. His fiance, Leah Kissinger, for her unwavering support and love. The incredible community of followers and supporters who have shared their passion and love of TTRPGs and helped him become a professional content creator. And to Adam, Alex, Brian, Nick, Sam, & Udo, his original adventuring party.

Inspirations

The NU system was originally inspired by games Joshua Orsak and his friends played using the 2nd Edition Dungeons and Dragons ruleset. It was further inspired by books on tabletop roleplaying game theory published in the early 90s, including the Idiot's Guide to TTRPGs.

Kurt Stridinger has also found inspiration in his love of TTRPGs, as well as his educational background in theater and storytelling.

Special Thanks

To our proofreaders: Chance Ryan, Curtis Haflett, Karafish 27, King Rubinsky, Sean Reynolds, Thaddeus Skye, Wyatt Giffis, & our editor Ryan Mossbargar.

As well as to the passionate community of players at the Orsak Narrative Universe who have helped to build, develop, and playtest the game and have indelibly left their mark upon it.

All artwork in this book has been professionally commissioned from Andersan Carman. Discover more at: www.andersoncarman.com

"We're all stories in the end…
Better make it a good one."